CHRIST EVANGELICAL BIBLE INSTITUTE

Revelation of Antichrist

Rev. Joseph Adam Pearson, Ph.D.

COPYRIGHT

Copyright © 2021 by Rev. Joseph Adam Pearson, Ph.D.

This work is a revision of these earlier versions copyrighted by the United States Copyright Office:

Copyright 2020 (TX-008-869-143)
Copyright 2018 (TX-008-565-606)
Copyright 2017 (TX-008-368-084)
Copyright 2014 (TX-008-056-307)
Copyright 2010 (TX-007-330-043)
Copyright 1989 (TX-003-516-271)
and Copyright 1981 (TXu-000-075-639)
by Joseph Adam Pearson.

All rights reserved.

Paper Book Identifiers:
ISBN-10: 0996222480
ISBN-13: 9780996222488

Published by
Christ Evangelical Bible Institute
(SAN: 920-3753)

Last edited on April 18, 2021
Dayton, Tennessee

DEDICATION

This work is dedicated to an untold number of persons who have already been — as well as those who are yet to be — terrorized and murdered by the workers of iniquity, chaos, and destruction for the sake of a false prophet whose name is eternally cursed (cbhnf*).

*(cbhnf) = cursed be his name forever

This work is also dedicated to the human beings who will be alive when the *only-begotten* Son of God, Christ Jesus, returns for his Millennial reign of peace on Earth. (By then, this world will have lost at least one-half of its population from warfare, lawlessness, famine, pestilence, plague, and cataclysmic disaster.)

FOREWORD

Dear Reader,

This book was written with the prompting and guidance of God's Holy Spirit and with the consent and encouragement of the Lord Jesus Christ himself. Therefore, the God of the Holy Bible deserves all praise for this book because it is He who has blessed me with salvation, spiritual gifts, wisdom, understanding, longevity, and spiritual success as well as all opportunities for education, personal growth, and Christian ministry. I am grateful for the Lord's decision to use me despite my considerable weaknesses, frailties, and vulnerabilities.

Concerning the Book of Revelation, what I have come to understand no human being has taught me (Galatians 1:12). God's Holy Spirit has been my only teacher. To be sure, God's Holy Spirit is the only teacher of truth (John 14:26). Because all good things come only from the God of the Holy Bible, I cannot boast to be the originator of the truth contained within this book. Although each of us may *discover* truth for ourselves, we *discover* it only because God *unveils* it to us in accordance with His Will, which is always pure, and with His timing, which is always perfect.

It is in the spirit of truth that I present this work to you so that many will be saved by being brought to the knowledge of salvation through understanding that the "testimony of Jesus Christ is the spirit of prophecy" (Revelation 19:10 KJV). *All* people need to know that they can stake their lives on the gospel truth contained within the Holy Bible and its Book of Revelation.

I pray that you take to heart the truth contained within this book and that you share this book with others. This book is not only a text of faith but also a test of faith.

Much love in Christ Jesus,

Joseph Adam Pearson

Rev. Joseph Adam Pearson, Ph.D.

P.S. Because this book needs to be available in pulp print through paper media to satisfy instructional requirements, this book is also available for purchase through *print-on-demand* at www.amazon.com. If you have not paid for this book because you have accessed it for free via its digital format, and if you would like to make a financial contribution, then please purchase paper copies of this book to distribute for free to others for them to read and study individually or in groups. All net profits from the sale of paper copies of this book go to support branch campuses of Christ Evangelical Bible Institute outside of the United States. If you like, you can also make contributions directly to Christ Evangelical Bible Institute to help promote global Bible education. Feel free to email the author at DrJPearson@aol.com.

P.P.S. Copies of this work in its original digital format may be made with the following provisions and stipulations: (1) This publication may be reproduced, stored in a retrieval system, and transmitted in any form and by any means (electronic, mechanical, photocopy, audio recording, or otherwise) but only as a complete work — without any changes — from its title page to its last page — (a) provided that it is NOT sold, bartered, exchanged and/or used to proselytize any particular Christian denomination (since the time for all division within the Body of Christ has drawn to a close) and (b) provided that commercial advertising is NOT superimposed on, in between, or around any of its pages. (2) This work may be translated into other languages provided that this original English version is appended to all digital translations. (3) Published paper copies of all translations must include facsimile copies of the original English title page, the original English copyright information page, and the pages of the original Foreword in English.

I encourage you to send digital as well as paper copies of this book to family, friends, colleagues, and others who might benefit from it. You also have my permission to post the entire book in its original format (i.e., exactly as it appears now) on your own web site or in other media formats that do not currently exist in 2020. However, except for your own personal copy, you must never post your own comments as "balloons" (i.e., captions) on any of its pages and you must not highlight any area for other readers. Finally, no one has the right to sell copies of this book except the author, his publishing company, and retail book stores that have purchased the book at its wholesale value.

NOTES

As used in this book, *KJV* is an abbreviation for the public domain *King James Version* of the Holy Bible. To ensure their accuracy throughout this book, all paraphrases of the public domain *King James Version* of the Holy Bible were finalized only after first checking: (1) the Masoretic Hebrew text of the Tanakh (the Jewish Bible) for accuracy of passages from the *KJV Old Testament* and (2) the earliest Greek text extant for accuracy of passages from the *KJV New Testament*. Additionally, to enhance readability of the public domain *KJV* text, words like *hath*, *thou*, and *ye* have been changed to their modern equivalents.

Most transliterated Hebrew and Greek words referenced within the text of this book are noted by their respective numbers [in brackets with a preceding "H" for Hebrew or "G" for Greek] from the *Dictionary of the Hebrew Bible* and the *Dictionary of the Greek Bible* found in *Strong's Exhaustive Concordance of the Bible* by James Strong (Copyright 1890), Crusade Bible Publishers, Inc., Nashville. Details for the majority of original Hebrew and Greek words indicated by numbers in brackets are provided by Table Two in Chapter Four of this book. A few additional Hebrew and Greek words are explained separately in other chapters as well as in Appendix A.

Although God the Father (i.e., the *Lord God Almighty*) and God the Son (i.e., the *Lord Jesus Christ*) are consubstantially united in the Godhead along with God the Holy Spirit, in order to distinguish *God the Father* from *God the Son*, an upper case "H" is used for personal pronouns specifically referring to *God the Father* (*He*, *His*, and *Him*) and a lower case "h" is used for personal pronouns specifically referring to *God the Son* (*he*, *his*, and *him*).

Whenever the word *God* is used in this book (i.e., with an upper case "G"), the reader should assume that the word is referring to the God of the Holy Bible — who is the *Lord God Almighty* or *Yahweh*

(YHWH), the one true and only real Creator-God. In contrast, whenever the word *god* is used in this book (i.e., with a lower case "g"), the reader should assume that the word is referring to the god of the Koran (al-Qur'an) — who is *not* the God of the Holy Bible. (How the two are different is explained in this book.)

Key words for external word search purposes include: Koran, Quran, Qur'an, al Qur'an, al-Qur'an, Antichrist, 666, Mohammed, Muhammad, Islamic State (IS), Islamic State of Iraq and Syria (ISIS), Islamic State of Iraq and al-Sham, Islamic State of Iraq and the Levant (ISIL), Al-Dawla Al-Islamiya fi al-Iraq wa al-Sham, Dawlat al-Islamiyah f'al-Iraq wa al-Sham, Daesh, DAIISH, Da'esh, Nusra Front, al-Qaeda, Hamas, Harakat al-Muqawama al-Islamiyya, Caliphate, Muslim Brotherhood, Hezbollah

......

For the sake of clarity, when the author of *Revelation of Antichrist* uses the phrase *the present author* in this book, he is referring to himself.

TABLE OF CONTENTS

Copyright	ii
Dedication	iii
Foreword	v
Notes	ix
Table of Contents	xi
Chapter One *Introduction*	1
Chapter Two *The Difference between Isaac and Ishmael*	7
Chapter Three *The Difference between Jesus and Mohammed*	15
Chapter Four *How It All Adds Up*	41
Chapter Five *Interpreting Prophecy in View of Islam*	63
Chapter Six *The Worst Woes*	87

Chapter Seven
Clarifications concerning the Antichrist — 101

Chapter Eight
The Fullness of Time — 103

Chapter Nine
Human Conflict — 119

Appendix A
Answers to Possible Questions about "666" — 133

Appendix B
The Seven Feasts of Israel — 139

Appendix C
Assumptions and Recommendations — 141

Appendix D
Instructor Guidelines — 149

Endnotes — 155

Afterword — 157

Books by the Author — 159

About the Author — 161

CHAPTER ONE
Introduction

Reading the Koran and the Holy Bible

The Koran (al-Qur'an), the book of Islam, is not only the testimony of a false prophet but also the testimony of Antichrist. Yet so many hearing that testimony today are willing to believe it, to take it to heart, to stand on it, and even to die for it as if it were written by the Spirit of Truth.

Have you ever read the Koran (al-Qur'an)? It is a book that has influenced almost as many people as the Holy Bible. It is a book that has contributed to the shaping of world history. And it is a book that will greatly influence the events of these last days. If you haven't, I recommend that you read it, but only after reading the Holy Bible first. Why? Though you may be able to spot absurdities in the Koran (al-Qur'an), you will not be able to see through the subtle elements of its powerful deception unless you first come to know and understand real Scripture (for the sake of clarity, the Holy Bible is the only real Scripture). Sure, it may take a while before you finish both, but don't you think you owe it to your own soul to at least look for the truth?

The whole premise is folly, you say? Then, consider this: If what I was writing supposedly unmasked the deceptions and myths of the Holy Bible, how many people would really care? And of those who would care, how many Christian believers would take it upon themselves to physically silence me? Though some might feel wounded or outraged and, perhaps, tempted to hurt me, I believe that

I would be able to pass through a crowd of them without harm. Could I say the same about Muslim believers if what I write defames the Koran (al-Qur'an)? No, it is dangerous to speak out against them, their society, their "prophet," and their so-called holy book. Few adherents of Islam tolerate any ideas other than their own, let alone dissent. Magnanimity is not a principle by which they operate. As demonstrated throughout the world today, Islam is irrevocably incompatible with freedom of speech and democratic values.

In the spirit of ecumenism, religious tolerance, or just not caring, many today have adopted a live-and-let-live attitude about spiritual beliefs. I, too, believe that there should be a freedom of choice concerning the way we define the Creator for ourselves and the way we worship the Creator. However, it is necessary for us to be aware that not everyone shares such ideals. In fact, very few people do. And there are those who would rob us of that right.

Until recently, Christians were most concerned about the threat that Communism poses to religious freedom. To them I say, you won't know real religious persecution until the Mohammedans have arrived. Mohammedans are opposed to religions other than their own because they feel they are a blasphemy to *Allah* — a blasphemy which is to be punished by them, at that.

Understanding the Book of Revelation

Bible specialists are sometimes unable to recognize overarching principles in the Holy Bible because they are too focused on the significance of details. On the other hand, Bible generalists are sometimes unable to recognize the significance of details because they are too focused on overarching principles. This is certainly true for those who try to read and study in order to comprehend prophetic Scripture found in the Book of Revelation.

Unless students of the Holy Bible read and reread prophetic Scripture while trying to hold its whole meaning at the same time they attend to its various details, either the significance of some of its details or some aspects of its overarching principles will not be recognized or remembered. To be sure, all authentic Christians remain students of the Holy Bible throughout their lives regardless of their status as ministerial practitioners or teachers of its written word.

What the Apostle John recorded as the Book of Revelation was received by him in a series of vignettes. Although he recorded the vignettes in the same series that he received them, not all the vignettes depict or refer to events that occur exactly in sequence. Although division of the Book of Revelation — indeed, the entire Bible — into chapters was originally done in the 13th century to help make the segmented text more easily digestible to the reader and, therefore, more fully comprehensible, the divisions are often artificial and, therefore, can mislead students into thinking that all events in each successive chapter are sequential when they are not. Consequently, one of the ways that I recommend that you proceed in your study of the Book of Revelation is to identify the various chapters as either (1) those that record events in sequence from one chapter to the next or (2) those that record events — even events that are also referred to in the chapters that depict sequential events — as a repetition of events recorded elsewhere for the sake of emphasis or clarification of how those events fit with other events that may occur sequentially or in tandem.

I came to understand overarching principles as well as details in the Book of Revelation as a result of:

1. Reading, rereading, and studying the entire Holy Bible.

2. Desiring to understand the prophecies contained in the Book of Revelation as well as the Book of Daniel.

3. Praying to the Lord God Almighty for insight and understanding.

4. Hearing an audible voice from Heaven that helped put me on the right

path of understanding by informing me that *"The worst woes will come to those who heap their grief by blood of sheep."*

5. Dreaming about end-time events and their details.

6. Having curiosity implanted within me by God about what the soul looks like.

7. Researching at a local college of Judaica what the soul might look like.

8. Discovering numerical ciphers, or codes, using the Hebrew alphabet.

9. Coming to understand that "666" is a cipher (i.e., code) for Mohammed (Muhammad).

10. Recognizing the truth concerning the role of the end-time Antichrist in relationship to:

    (a) the world religion known as Islam,

    (b) the false god known as *Allah*,

    (c) the deceptive nature of the Koran (al-Qur'an), and

    (d) the extent of the depravity of its original false prophet.

Students of the Book of Revelation have a responsibility to God and to others to "study to show themselves approved unto God" (2 Timothy 2:15 KJV Paraphrase). They also have a responsibility to God and to themselves to not incur the Wrath of God by changing prophetic elements in the Book of Revelation:

{18} For I [Jesus] testify unto every person who hears the words of the prophecy of this book [i.e., the Book of Revelation]: If anyone shall add unto these things, God shall add unto that person the plagues that are written in this book [i.e., the Book of Revelation]. {19} And if any person shall take away from the words of the book of this prophecy [i.e., the Book of Revelation],

God shall take away that person's part out of the book of life, and out of the holy city, and in the things that are written in this book [i.e., the Book of Revelation].

Revelation 22:18-19 KJV (Paraphrase)

Thus, concerning the Book of Revelation, (1) although it is alright to change words like "man" to "person" or "human being" because "person" and "human being" capture the intended meaning from the original text; and (2) although it is alright to change figurative phrases like "kidneys and hearts" (from the Greek of Revelation 2:23) to "minds and hearts" because the phrase "minds and hearts" captures the intended meaning from the original text; and (3) although it is alright for us to offer our interpretations of its prophetic elements in brackets or parentheses embedded in its quoted verses [as the present author has done in the previous quote], one cannot add unintended meaning or subtract intended meaning from the Book of Revelation without invoking one of the two curses of God recorded in Revelation 22:18-19.

As a side note here, I have purposely included "the Book of Revelation" four times in brackets in the previous quote of Revelation 22:18-19 to emphasize that the two curses are specifically associated with the Book of Revelation and not with the entire Bible as some Bible students have erroneously claimed.

In the final analysis, let us all take care not to speak for God or to put words in His mouth or say that He has not said what He has said. Let us all take care not to offend God.

CHAPTER TWO

Isaac and Ishmael

In the Koran (al-Qur'an), the followers of Mohammed are instructed to say:

> We believe in [Allah], and that which has been sent down on us, and sent down on Abraham and Ishmael, Isaac and Jacob, and the Tribes [of Israel], and in that which was given to Moses and Jesus, and the prophets, of their Lord; we make no division between [i.e., distinction among] any of them, and to [Allah] we surrender.
>
> *Surah 3.084*[1]

Capable students of the Bible will recognize the subtle introduction of Ishmael into the lineage of those who received the covenant of God. They will recall that Ishmael was the son of Abraham and Hagar — the handmaid, or bondswoman, of Sarah. They will remember that, concerning Ishmael, it was prophesied through the angel of the Lord: "he will be a wild man [or, closer to the Hebrew, "a wild ass of a man"]; his hand will be against every man, and every man's against him" (Genesis 6:12 KJV). And they will remember that it was only through Isaac that God was to establish His Covenant, not through Ishmael (see Genesis 17:18-22).

In reality, Ishmael and Hagar were to become outcasts — banished by Abraham with God's approval (Genesis 21:9-12). That Ishmael was disinherited is reaffirmed when God later commands Abraham to take his "*only* son" Isaac (Genesis 22: 2, 12, and 16 KJV). After banishment, Ishmael is mentioned little more than in genealogies (Genesis 25:9-17 and 1 Chronicles 1:28-31) and in his alliance with the disinherited son of Isaac, Esau — which alliance is signified through the marriage of Esau to Mahalath, Ishmael's daughter (Genesis 28:9).

God said plainly: "I WILL ESTABLISH MY COVENANT WITH HIM [ISAAC] FOR AN EVERLASTING COVENANT, AND WITH HIS SEED AFTER HIM" (Genesis 17:19 KJV); "MY COVENANT WILL I ESTABLISH WITH ISAAC" (Genesis 17:21 KJV); and "LET IT NOT BE GRIEVOUS IN YOUR [ABRAHAM'S] SIGHT BECAUSE OF THE BOY [ISHAMEL], AND BECAUSE OF THE BONDWOMAN... FOR IN ISAAC SHALL THY SEED BE CALLED" (Genesis 21:12 KJV).

However, in spite of all that is recorded in the Holy Bible, Mohammed attempted to vindicate and elevate Ishmael's status:

> And We [the word "We" in the Koran (al-Qur'an) is often used to denote Allah speaking**] made covenant with Abraham and Ishmael...
>
> *Surah 2.125* [2]

** When used by one person or for one entity, the first person plural (i.e., "we") is sometimes referred to as the "royal we," "majestic plural" (Latin *pluralis maiestatis*) or "plural of excellence" (Latin *pluralis excellentiae*). Muslims would explain that, although Allah is one being, their deity scripted the Qur'an with "we" (Arabic *nahnu* نحن or one of its affix derivatives) to denote a higher position of authority than the first person singular pronoun "I." Thus, although in plural form, the word "we" here is not being used to denote more than one being or person but, instead, royalty, majesty, and authority. The use of plural for one person can be found in a number of global languages, including others in the Middle East.

For Christian monarchs, including the Roman Catholic Popes (especially before John Paul II), "we" is sometimes used to mean that the person has God's mind (i.e., knows His Will) on certain matters as a "divine right." *For example,* some kings of England considered themselves not only heads of state but heads of the church of Christ as God's chosen representatives on Earth; therefore, when they issued an edict, they might state: "*We* find that . . ." or "*We* decree that . . ." Although many Protestants think that the Pope is always considered infallible by his clergy and congregation, that is not so in actual practice. The Pope only *invokes* infallibility on occasion; and, when he does, he might use the Latin *nos* ("we") to denote that he is functioning as God's representative here on Earth.

And mention in the Book Ishmael; he was true to his promise, and he was a Messenger, a Prophet. He bade his people to pray and give alms, and he was pleasing to [Allah].

Surah 19.054-.055 [3]

Today, partly because of such false justifications in the Koran (al-Qur'an), all Muslims proudly call upon Abraham as their progenitor through Ishmael. Muslims have accepted the teaching of Mohammed that:

No; Abraham in truth was not a Jew, neither a Christian; but he was a Muslim and one pure of faith...

Surah 3.067 [4]

O men, bow you down and prostrate yourselves, and serve your Lord, and do good; haply so you shall prosper; and struggle for [Allah] as is his due, for he has chosen you, and has laid on you no impediment in your religion, being the creed of your father Abraham; [Allah] named you Muslims aforetime and in this, that the Messenger might be a witness against you, and that you might be witnesses against mankind.

Surah 22.078 [5]

Following is what the Apostle Paul said concerning Isaac and Ishmael:

For it is written that Abraham had two sons: one by a bondwoman and one by a freewoman. The one who was of the bondwoman was born after the flesh; but the one of the freewoman was by promise. These things are an allegory concerning two covenants; one from mount Sinai, which gives birth

---

As the author of the Qur'an, Satan is merely impersonating, aping, and mocking the real Lord God Almighty when he uses "we."

to bondage, which is represented by Hagar. Hagar, in turn, represents Mount Sinai in Arabia, and answers to Jerusalem which now is, and is in bondage with her children. But Jerusalem which is above us is free, which is the mother of us all. For it is written: "Rejoice you barren who does not give birth; break forth and cry, you who travail not: for the desolate has many more children than she who has a husband." Now we, brothers and sisters, as Isaac was, are the children of promise. But as he who was born after the flesh persecuted him who was born after the Spirit, even so it is now. Nevertheless what does the Scripture say? Cast out the bondwoman and her son: for the son of the bondwoman shall not be heir with the son of the freeman. So then, brothers and sisters, we are not children of the bondwoman, but of the free.

Galatians 4:22-31 KJV (Paraphrase)

I believe the allegory that Paul cited is a far greater figure of things than most people think. I believe that the allegory, not only helps us to understand such things as spiritual freedom and spiritual bondage and the persecution that the spiritually-minded must suffer at the hand of the carnally-minded, but also provides Christians with the key to a final separation among the "children of men" (i.e., human beings) — a separation between those who believe on the one who came in the Father's name (Jesus Christ) and those who believe on the one who came (1) in his own name (Mohammed) and (2) in the name of the Enemy of the one true and only real God (which Enemy is Satan himself).

The entirety of Islam is but a parody of the truth — a parody that both literally and figuratively tries to tear down the structure that God has built to rebuild another in its place. For what reason? So the foundation God laid and the cornerstone He established, that lost souls might be returned to Him, could be obscured from their view.

Consider what has happened in Jerusalem on Mount Moriah.

Mount Moriah is the place where Abraham, as a test of faith, was ordered by God to sacrifice his son Isaac instead of a lamb as a burnt offering (see Genesis 22:1-14), — the same place where King David was instructed by an angel through the seer Gad to "set up an altar unto the Lord" (read 1 Chronicles 21:18-30 and 22:1-11; 2 Samuel 24:18-25), — and the very same place where "Solomon began to build the house of the Lord [i.e., the Jerusalem Temple]" (2 Chronicles 3:1 KJV).

Islam has tried to pervert and subvert the selection of the site for the establishment of God's Jerusalem Temple in two ways: First, Muslim tradition has it that prior to Abraham's above-mentioned test with Isaac he was similarly tested with Ishmael at Mecca[6] and that, after passing the test, both he and Ishmael built the Kaaba, which structure Islam claims is the first house ever made for the worship of God — such house now contained within the court of the Great Mosque of Mecca in Saudi Arabia. (However, to the one true God, who is the God of the Holy Bible, the Kaaba is only a spiritual outhouse for the unclean.) Second, Muslims claim the site of Solomon's Temple as their own holy place. In fact, the Dome of the Rock (the so-called Mosque of Omar) was built in 691-692 A.D. over the rock that is believed to have been a part of the great altar used for burnt offerings within the first Jerusalem Temple.

Concerning this matter of the house of the Lord God Almighty, the Apostle Paul further helps us to identify Islam as a major component in the great "falling away" (2 Thessalonians 2:3 KJV) by stating that in the latter times Satan would be revealed as he "who opposes and exalts himself above all that is called God, or that is worshiped; so that he as God sits in the temple of God, showing himself that he is God" (2 Thessalonians 2:4 KJV).

True, the Temple of God today is His Church and His Church is the Body of Christ, but also true is that in this world darkness tries to obscure the truth to confuse human beings and the issue of salvation as much as possible. And the site of Solomon's Temple is important to the Devil not only for the reason of replacing truth with error but also because there is still to be a third Jewish temple built upon the Temple

Mount in Jerusalem to fulfill Bible prophecy (Daniel 9:24-27).

It is evident to me that the Devil — "the god of this world" (2 Corinthians 4:4 KJV) — has tried to remove the light of truth within the Old and New Testaments by attempting to rewrite history and Scripture through the appearance of Mohammed as a prelude to the appearance of the final Antichrist in these end-times.

Concerning Islam's claim that Abraham traveled with Ishmael to Mecca, Alfred Guillame, a noted Professor of Arabic and Islamic studies, states that "there is no historical evidence for the assertion that Abraham or Ishmael was ever in Mecca, and if there had been such a tradition it would have to be explained how all memory of the Old Semitic name *Ishmael* (which was not in its true Arabian form in Arabian inscriptions and written correctly with an initial consonant Y) came to be lost. The form in the Koran (al-Qur'an) is taken either from Greek or Syriac sources."[7]

Dr. Guillame adds that many words in the Koran (al-Qur'an) do not yield a meaning unless they are traced back to their Hebrew or Syriac sources, and that this is especially important in view of the fact that the Koran (al-Qur'an) purports itself to have been written in pure and unadulterated Arabic.

For proof that Mohammed tried to rewrite Scripture, all we need do is compare a few central teachings in the Bible with those in the Koran (al-Qur'an):

1. Christ Jesus said to his followers: "In the world you shall have tribulation" (John 16:33 KJV). Mohammed said: "Those who believe and are godfearing — for them is good tidings in the present life"[8] and "The present life is nothing but a sport and a diversion."[9]

2. The Apostle Paul wrote: "By grace are you saved through faith …

not of works, so that no man should boast" (Ephesians 2:9 KJV). Mohammed wrote that [Allah] created this world "— that he might try you, which one of you is fairer in works."[10]

3. The Bible teaches that we are responsible for our own failings. Mohammed says: "And my sincere counsel will not profit you, if I desire to counsel you sincerely, if [Allah] desires to pervert you."[11] [God does not tempt or pervert human beings!]

4. Compare the Bible's "Let no man say when he is tempted, I am tempted of God: for God cannot be tempted with evil, neither tempts He any man" (James 1:13 KJV) to the Koran's "[Allah] leads astray whomever he will"[12] and "We try you with evil and good for a testing."[13]

5. Compare these words of Christ Jesus concerning the woman taken in adultery: "He who is without sin among you, let him cast the first stone" (John 8:7 KJV) with these words of Mohammed: "The fornicatress and the fornicator — scourge each one of them a hundred stripes, and in the matter of [Allah's] religion let no tenderness seize you if you believe in [Allah] and the last Day; and let a party of believers witness their chastisement."[14]

6. Christ Jesus said: "My kingdom is not of this world" (John 18:36 KJV). Mohammed, however, testified of a sensuous heaven wherein are "the Houris" — beautiful nymphs that are among the rewards for faithful Muslims. He says: "Surely for the godfearing awaits a place of security, gardens, vineyards, and maidens with swelling breasts, like of age, and a cup overflowing."[15]

7. Finally, Christ Jesus said that, in Heaven, we "neither marry, nor are given in marriage, but are as angels of God in Heaven" (Matthew 22:30 KJV). In contradiction to Christ Jesus, Mohammed said that "the inhabitants of Paradise today are busy in their rejoicing; they and their spouses, reclining upon couches in the shade."[16] [The Holy Bible is clear that we neither marry nor have sexual intercourse in Heaven!]

CHAPTER THREE
Jesus and Mohammed

Contrasting the Bible and the Koran

Jesus' birth as *the Messiah* was prophesied in Scripture. (As stated earlier, the Holy Bible is the only Scripture.) Mohammed's birth as the so-called *Seal of the Prophets* was never prophesied in the Bible.

Through many witnesses, the Holy Spirit established the lineage of the Christ (i.e., the Messiah or H'Moshiach) from Abraham through Isaac and Jacob to the tribe of Judah and out of the house of David (Genesis 12:3, 18:18, 21:12, 22:18, 26:4, 28:14, 49:10; 2 Samuel 7:12-16; Psalms 18:50, 89:3-4, 89:20, 132:11; Isaiah 9:6-7, 11:1, 11:10; Jeremiah 23:5-6, 33:14-15). Moreover, it was prophesied through Isaiah that the Messiah would be conceived by a virgin (Isaiah 7:14). It was prophesied through Micah that he would be born in Bethlehem (Micah 5:2). And it was prophesied through the typology in the third and sixth chapters of Zechariah that his name would be Yehoshuah [H3091] — from which the Ionic Greek form "Iesous" [G2424] is derived, the Classical Latin form "Iesus" [IESVS] is derived, and the Early Modern English "Jesus" is derived. (Details for the original Hebrew and Greek words indicated by numbers in brackets are provided by Table Two in the Fourth Chapter of this book.)

Who prophesied the birth of Mohammed as a true prophet of God? No one. No one except Mohammed. Mohammed wrote:

Jesus son of Mary said, "Children of Israel, I am indeed the Messenger of [Allah] to you, confirming the Torah that is before me, and giving good tidings of a Messenger who shall come after me, whose name shall be Ahmed."

Surah 61.006 [17]

There is no record in the Holy Bible that the Lord Jesus said any such thing!

Throughout the Koran (al-Qur'an), Mohammed refutes that Jesus Christ was the Son of God:

The Messiah, Jesus son of Mary, was only the Messenger of [Allah], and [Allah's] Word that [Allah] committed to Mary, and a spirit from [Allah].

Surah 4.171 [18]

The Messiah, son of Mary, was only a Messenger; Messengers before him passed away; his mother was a just woman; they both ate food. Behold, how We make clear signs to them; then behold, how they are perverted!

Surah 5.075 [19]

The Creator of the heavens and the earth — how should He have a Son, seeing that He has no consort, and He created all things, and He has knowledge of everything?

Surah 6.101 [20]

The Jews say, "Ezra is the Son of God;" the Christians say, "The Messiah is the Son of God." That is the utterance of their mouths, confirming with the unbelievers before them.

Surah 9.030 [21]

They [the Christians] say, "God has taken to Him a son." Glory be to Him! He is All-sufficient; to Him belongs all that is in the heavens and in the earth; you have no authority for this. What, so you say concerning [Allah] that you know not? Say: "Those who forge against [Allah] falsehood shall not prosper. Some enjoyment in this world; then unto Us they shall return; then We shall let them taste the terrible chastisement, for that they were unbelievers [in Mohammed and the Koran]."

Surah 10.068-070 [22]

Praise belongs to [Allah], who has not taken to him a son.

Surah 17.111 [23]

And they say, "The All-merciful has taken unto Himself a son." You have indeed advanced something hideous! The heavens are well-nigh rent of it and the earth split asunder, and the mountains well-nigh fall down crashing for they have attributed to the All-merciful a son; and it behooves not the All-merciful to take a son.

Surah 19.088-092 [24]

[Allah] has not taken to himself any son.

Surah 23.091 [25]

[Allah] has not taken to him a son.

Surah 25.002 [26]

Is it not of their own calumny that they say, "God has begotten?" They are truly liars.

Surah 37.151-152 [27]

And when the son of Mary is cited as an example, behold, your people turn away from it and say, "What are our gods better, or he?" They [the Christians] cite him [Jesus] not to thee, except to dispute; nay, but they are a people contentious. He is only a servant We blessed, and We made him to be an example to the Children of Israel.

Surah 43.057-059 [28]

It was Mohammed's self-proclaimed mission "...to warn those who say, 'God has taken to Himself a son.'"[29] However, many have testified of the Messiah's Sonship: It was prophesied by God's Holy Spirit through King David: "I will be his father, and he shall be my son" (2 Samuel 7:14 KJV). Through Isaiah: "Unto us a child is born, unto us a son is given" (Isaiah 9:6 KJV). Through the Angel Gabriel to Mary: "He shall be great, and shall be called the Son of the Highest" (Luke 1:32 KJV) and "The Holy Ghost shall come upon you [Mary]: therefore also that holy thing which shall be born of you shall be called 'the Son of God'" (Luke 1:35 KJV). John the Baptist bore record that Jesus was the Son of God (John 1:32-34). God Himself testified twice of Jesus: "THIS IS MY BELOVED SON, IN WHOM I AM WELL PLEASED" (Matthew 3:17, 17:5; Mark 1:11, 9:7; and Luke 3:22, 9:35 KJV). Saint Mark testified in his gospel: "Jesus Christ, the Son of God" (Mark 1:1 KJV). The bedrock of the Christian faith is found in the Apostle Peter's declaration to Jesus: "You are the Christ, the Son of the Living God" (Matthew 16:16 KJV).

Even the unclean spirits recognized that Jesus Christ was the Son of God: "And, behold, they [the unclean spirits] cried out, saying, 'What have we to do with you, Jesus, you Son of God? Are you come here to torment us before the time [of the Final Judgment]?'" (Matthew 8:29 KJV Paraphrase)[30]

To casual observers and lifeless Christians, that Mohammed claimed God had no Son in Jesus does not seem to be so very damaging: after all, they think, Mohammed did acknowledge that Jesus was a prophet, "a Messenger of God." These fail to see that for Mohammed to have stated that Jesus was not a prophet would have kept many from his own false teachings; it would have prevented their even listening to Mohammed's message. Further, these fail to see that Mohammed had to include Jesus within his teachings if he was to be more convincing concerning his own authority. Why? It is easier to deceive if you pretend to build on an already-established foundation of truth. It is easier to convince your enemy that you are his friend if you pretend to honor what he believes. And truth is easier to destroy in the mind of the believer if you claim your heritage in truth:

> Surely We sent down the Torah, wherein is guidance and light, thereby the Prophets who had surrendered themselves gave judgment for those of Jewry, as did the masters and the rabbis, following such portion of God's Book as they were given to keep and were witness to... And We sent, following in their footsteps, Jesus son of Mary, confirming the Torah before him; and We gave to him the Gospel, wherein is guidance and light, and confirming the Torah before it, as a guidance and an admonition unto the godfearing.
>
> *Surah 5.044 & 046* [31]

Mohammed tries to persuade us that the Koran (al-Qur'an) is just as scriptural as the Torah (i.e., the Law, or *Instruction*, of Moses) and the New Testament Gospels. He tries to make it seem as if the Torah and the Gospels and the Koran (al-Qur'an) are all equal parts in a threefold plan of divine revelation to humankind. Why? The most effective way to win individuals over to your way of thinking is to, first, tell them what they already believe is true (so you don't alienate them) and, second, slowly persuade them that what they don't yet know or understand can be provided for, or answered by, your doctrines: This is the effective *wolf-in-shepherd's-clothing approach.* Indeed, in the charade of a religion named *Islam*, Satan has proved himself to be the master saboteur by duping at least one-fourth of the world's population into honoring him rather than the God of the Holy Bible.

Both Moses and Jesus proved their words with works and signs following. The miracles performed through them proved the truths they spoke and the lives they lived. Christ Jesus said:

> ...for the works which the Father has given me to finish, the same works that I do, bear witness of me, that the Father has sent me.
>
> *John 5:36 KJV*

Jesus also said:

> Say you of him, whom the Father has sanctified, and sent into the world, "You blaspheme;" because I said, "I am the Son of God"? If I do not the works of my Father, believe me not. But if I do, though you believe not me, believe the works: that you may know, and believe, that the Father is in me, and I in Him.
>
> *John 10:36-38 KJV*

Mohammed did not prove his words with works. Oh, he frequently proclaims that the Surahs (the main divisions or chapters) of the Koran (al-Qur'an) are themselves "signs, clear signs." But there are no accounts of miracles wrought through Mohammed except unreliable accounts that are attributed to him through the imagination and invention of his followers. Mohammed tried to explain away the absence of such proofs this way:

> They say, "Why have signs not been sent down upon him from his Lord?" Say: "The signs are only with [Allah], and I am only a plain warner." What, is it not sufficient for them that We have sent down upon thee the Book that is recited to them [meaning the Koran]? Surely, in that is a mercy, and a reminder to a people who believe.
>
> *Surah 29.050-051* [32]

> It is [Allah] who has sent his Messenger [Mohammed] with the guidance and the religion of truth, that he may uplift it above every religion. [Allah] suffices as a witness.
>
> *Surah 48.028* [33]

Mohammed claimed that it was only for him to deliver "the Message Manifest," the final word from God.[34] In this way, he tried to delude people into thinking that he superseded and supplanted Jesus Christ. In doing so, the Devil seeks to establish his authority for overturning the principles of peace, love, and forgiveness taught by the one true and only real Savior.

Christ Jesus instructed us to love our enemies, to curse not when we are cursed, to forgive those who despitefully use us, and to refrain from judging others, or condemning our peers. Hear what Mohammed had to say on those topics:

O believers, prescribed for you is retaliation, touching the slain; freeman for freeman, slave for slave, female for female... In retaliation there is life for you, men possessed of minds; haply you will be godfearing.
Surah 2.178-179 [35]

And fight in the way of [Allah] with those who fight with you.... And slay them wherever you come upon them, and expel them from where they expelled you; [your own] persecution is more grievous than slaying [others].
Surah 2.191 [36]

Whoso commits aggression against you, do you commit aggression against him like as he has committed against you...
Surah 2.194 [37]

Prescribed for you is fighting, though it be hateful to you.
Surah 2.216 [38]

...take not to yourselves friends of them [the unbelievers] until they emigrate in the way of [Allah]; then, if they turn their backs, take them, and slay them wherever you find them...
Surah 4.089 [39]

This is the recompense of those who fight against [Allah] and his messenger [Mohammed], and hasten about the earth, to do corruption there: they shall be slaughtered, or crucified, or their hands and feet shall alternately be struck off, or they shall be banished from the land.
Surah 5.033 [40]

Fight them [the unbelievers], till there is no persecution and the religion is [Allah's] entirely.

Surah 8.039 [41]

It is not for any Prophet to have prisoners until he make wide slaughter in the land.

Surah 8.067 [42]

Slay the idolaters wherever you find them, and take them, and confine them, and lie in wait for them at every place of ambush.

Surah 9.005 [43]

Fight those who believe not in [Allah] and the Last Day.

Surah 9.029 [44]

And fight the unbelievers totally even as they fight you totally; and know that [Allah] is with the godfearing.

Surah 9.036 [45]

O believers, fight the unbelievers who are near to you, and let them find in you a harshness; and know that [Allah] is with the godfearing.

Surah 9.123 [46]

The recompense of evil is evil the like of it...

Surah 42.040 [47]

When you meet the unbelievers, smite their necks [slash their throats or behead them], then, when you have made wide slaughter among them, tie fast the bonds; then set them free, either by grace or ransom, till the war lays down its loads.

Surah 47.004 [48]

Mohammed is the Messenger of [Allah], and those who are with him are hard against the unbelievers, merciful one to another.

Surah 48.029 [49]

Thou shalt not find any people who believe in [Allah] and the Last Day who are loving to anyone who opposes [Allah] and his Messenger.

Surah 58.022 [50]

O Prophet, struggle with the unbelievers and the hypocrites, and be thou harsh with them.

Surah 66.009 [51]

It should be clear that the literature of Mohammed is hateful, encouraging people to live both in fear and by the sword in judgment of one another. Compare the preceding quotations with the following instructions given to us by Jesus the Christ:

"But I say unto you who hear, 'Love your enemies, do good to them who hate you, Bless them who curse you, and pray for them who despitefully use you. And unto him that smites you on the one cheek offer also the other; and him that takes away your cloke forbid not to take thy coat also. Give to every man who asks of thee; and of him that takes away your goods ask for them not again. And as you would have that men should do to you, do you also to them likewise. For if you love them who love you, what thanks have you? for sinners also love those that love them. And if you do good to them who do good to you, what thanks have you? for sinners also do the same. And if you lend to them of whom you hope to receive, what thanks have you? for sinners also lend to sinners, to receive as much again. But love you your enemies, and do good, and lend, hoping for nothing again; and your reward shall be great, and you shall be the children of the Highest: for He is kind unto the unthankful and to the evil. Be you therefore merciful, as your Father also is merciful. Judge not, and you shall not be judged, condemn not, and you shall not be condemned: forgive, and you shall be forgiven: Give, and it shall be given unto you; good measure, pressed down, and shaken together, and running over, shall men give into your bosom. For with the same measure that you give out, so shall it be measured to you again.'"

Luke 6:27-38 KJV

After comparing the previous passage from the Holy Bible with those immediately preceding it from the Koran (al-Qur'an), which one of the two — Jesus or Mohammed — do you think is the true witness of our loving, heavenly Father?

Considering what is written in the Koran (al-Qur'an), there should be little wonder why Bibles are not allowed into many countries over which the banner of Islam flies. The people of those nations might be able to read:

Thus says the Lord: **SUCH AS ARE FOR DEATH, TO DEATH: AND SUCH AS ARE FOR THE SWORD, TO THE SWORD: AND SUCH AS ARE FOR THE FAMINE, TO THE FAMINE: AND SUCH AS ARE FOR THE CAPTIVITY, TO THE CAPTIVITY.**

Jeremiah 15:2 KJV

Put up again your sword into its place: for all who take the sword shall perish with the sword.

Matthew 26:52 KJV

He that leads into captivity shall go into captivity: he that kills with the sword must be killed with the sword.

Revelation 13:10 KJV

Dearly beloved, avenge not yourselves, but rather, give place unto [God's] wrath: for it is written, **VENGEANCE IS MINE; I WILL REPAY,** says the Lord. Therefore if your enemy is hungry, then feed him; if he thirsts, then give him something to drink; for in so doing you shall heap coals of fire on his head. Be not overcome with evil, but overcome evil with good.

Romans 12:19-21 KJV

In short, they (i.e., the people of nations over which the banner of Islam flies) would find out that the God of Abraham, Isaac, and Jacob — the one of whom Christ Jesus came to testify — is the God of peace and love and not the god of war, terror, and hatred. Moreover, they would learn of the Levitical high priest and his role as intercessor for the children of Israel, offering sacrifice once a year for their sins, and how Christ Jesus was sent to sacrifice himself "once for all" (Hebrews 10:10 KJV). They would learn how the Old Testament events, rules, and regulations were but a figure, or typology, of things to come. They would learn to understand the role of the Lamb of God, Jesus Christ, as Intercessor for *all nations* under the Sun. And, finally, concerning their relationship to Christ Jesus, they would learn that "there is no other name under heaven given among men and women, whereby we must be saved" (Acts 4:12 KJV).

Throughout the Koran (al-Qur'an), Mohammed attempts to refute the role of Christ Jesus as the *only-begotten* Son of God and only Savior of the world. He tries to negate that the Lamb "bare the sin of many, and made intercession for the transgressors" (Isaiah 53:12 KJV) and that "he ever lives to make intercession for them" (Hebrews 7:25 KJV):

Intercessor there is none, except after [Allah's] leave.
Surah 10.003 [52]

...no intercessors shall they have amongst their associates, and they shall disbelieve in their associates.
Surah 30.013 [53]

Intercession will not avail with [Allah] save for him to whom [Allah] gives leave.
Surah 34.023 [54]

To [Allah] belongs intercession altogether.
Surah 39.044 [55]

...the evildoers [those who do not believe in Mohammed and the Koran] have not one loyal friend, no intercessor to be heeded.
Surah 40.018 [56]

...no soul laden bears the load of another.
Surah 53.038 [57]

Come, now, and [Allah's] Messenger [Mohammed] will ask forgiveness for you.
Surah 63.005 [58]

It is plain that Mohammed tried to set himself up in place of Christ Jesus. What of the crucifixion? Mohammed denies that Christ Jesus was in a flesh body at the time of the crucifixion:

...they did not slay him, neither crucified him, only a likeness of that was shown to them.
Surah 4.157 [59]

Guilty of the ultimate crime against God are those who steadfastly maintain that Jesus Christ is not the *only-begotten* Son of God and that he did not die for our sins. For that reason alone, Mohammed condemns himself and his followers (as long as they remain his followers). The Lord Jesus said:

"For God so loved the world that He gave His *only begotten* Son, that whoever believes in him should not perish, but have everlasting life. For God sent not His Son into the world to condemn the world; but that the world through him might be saved. He that believes on him is not condemned: but he that believes not is condemned already, because he has not believed in the name of the only begotten Son of God."
John 3:16-18 KJV

"I am come in my Father's name, and you receive me not: if another shall come in his own name, him you shall receive."
John 5:43 KJV

"If I had not come and spoken unto them, they had not had sin: but now they have no cloke for their sin. He that hates me hates my Father also. If I had not done among them the works which no other man did, they had not had sin: but now have they both seen and hated both me and my Father."
John 15:22-24 KJV

The greatest lie in this world is that Jesus Christ is not the *only-begotten* Son of God:

Who is a liar but he or she who denies that Jesus is the Christ? That person is antichrist who denies the Father and the Son.
1 John 2:22 KJV

What is the destiny of such liars?

… all liars shall have their part in the lake [i.e., "the Lake of Fire"] that burns with fire and brimstone, which lake is the second death.
Revelation 21:8 KJV

Simply stated, without Christ Jesus we have no *advocate* with God the Father. If we reject the one God has sent, we reject the mercy He extends to us through that one.

Muslims might argue that Jesus Christ is the son of God to the same degree that all human beings are "sons of God" (i.e., "children of God"). They fail to realize that, as the *only-begotten* Son of God (John 3:16), Jesus Christ has a singularly unique place in the entire history of the human race (past, present, and future) because he is the only human being ever conceived directly by God's Holy Spirit in consort with a human mother. In other words, no human father was directly or indirectly involved in the conception of Jesus Christ. In the language of the Holy Bible, no human father "begat" him (i.e., provided the seed, or sperm, for his birth).

Jesus Christ is the *only-begotten* Son of God. If you and I are ever faced with a choice between acknowledging that Jesus Christ is the *only-begotten* Son of God or our own beheading (Revelation 20:4), I pray that our Lord's strength be within us and upon us so that we never refute this absolute, unequivocal, and eternal truth. Although our heads might be severed from our bodies, authentic Christian believers can never be severed from the Body of Christ if they remain true to the *only-begotten* Son of God.

Why is it so important for Satan to keep human beings from understanding that Jesus Christ is the *only-begotten* Son of God? Satan keeps them from accepting eternal salvation. Why does Satan rage against Christians? Satan rages because he is so full of envy and because he hates the Lord God Almighty and seeks to rob Him of His creation. Although Satan can "ape," imitate, or mimic the one true and only real God in many ways, Satan is only an illusionist. Although Satan can spawn like-minded individuals through his cunning, evil, and hatred, he can never conceive a human being. Satan cannot create. Satan can only make monsters from the spiritually dead. Moreover, Satan seeks to deny human beings eternal salvation because eternal salvation is something he himself cannot receive.

Unfortunately, Satan keeps many Muslims from accepting that Jesus Christ is the *only-begotten* Son of God because Satan convinces them through the Koran (al-Qur'an) that:

1. God is all-sufficient and does not need an *only-begotten* Son.

2. The Christian concept of "God the Father, God the Son, and God the Holy Spirit" is polytheistic and, therefore, against

the monotheistic nature of God. (Authentic Christian believers who embrace the phraseology *"God the Father, God the Son, and God the Holy Spirit"* do not believe in "three Gods." They believe in the one true and only real God.)

3. Because God is all-powerful (i.e., omnipotent), God does not need an *only-begotten* Son to save human beings if He desires to save them.

Mohammed really thought that the Angel Gabriel (a true Messenger of God) appeared to him and gradually dictated the Koran (al-Qur'an) to him over a period of more than twenty years. Mohammed did not know that it was Satan who had presented himself as "an angel of light" (2 Corinthians 11:14 KJV) to him. And Mohammed did not know that it was Satan who had invisibly recited the Koran (al-Qur'an) to him.

Mohammed was the perfect choice as Satan's prophet for the following reasons:

1. Mohammed was not a Christian and, therefore, did not have God's Holy Spirit residing within him. Without God's Holy Spirit residing within him, Mohammed could not distinguish between good and evil. He had no way of knowing that the angel was Satan and not Gabriel.

2. Mohammed did not understand that the Holy Bible is the only real Scripture. Therefore, Mohammed could not recognize that what was being recited to him was a pack of lies dictated by Satan. Because he did not know spiritual truth, he could not recognize spiritual falsehood. All Mohammed believed was that it was an invisible heavenly creature who was speaking to him.

3. Mohammed was psychologically unstable. He wanted to believe that he was prophet material when he clearly was not.

He fancied himself a prophet. Unfortunately, he did not recognize that he would only be a false prophet. He was a tool and a pawn. He was used by Satan. All Mohammed could think was that he had been chosen by the one true and only real God. He did not know that it was Satan and not the Lord God Almighty who had chosen him. Because such phenomenal supernatural events occurred within Mohammed's life, and because he was not grounded by God's written word in the Holy Bible, Mohammed became increasingly passionate and fanatical about broadcasting the words spoken to him by Satan. His fanaticism helped to spread the written lie known as the Koran (al-Qur'an). His fanaticism continues in his followers, especially evident today in Islamists, Jihadists, and Salafists and their associated organizations.

Mohammed did not understand that Satan is a liar, that Satan is the father of lying, and that Satan's native language is lying (John 8:44). Mohammed did not understand that Satan only speaks lies. Satan speaks lies by distorting the truth and disguising evil. In fact, Satan is the originator of deception, disinformation, misinformation, diversion, and fake news — all intended to reframe the good news of salvation through Jesus Christ so that unsaved people might be misled and, thereby, detoured away from receiving and accepting the gospel message of salvation through Jesus Christ.

Mohammed did not know that Satan cannot bear the truth that Jesus Christ is the *only-begotten* Son of God. Mohammed did not understand Satan's cunning and depraved nature. To be sure, Mohammed did not fabricate the Koran (al-Qur'an). It was Satan who spoke the passages of the Koran (al-Qur'an) to him. Regardless of whether Mohammed was literate or illiterate and did the transcriptions himself or had someone else do them, Mohammed was still a "fool" in the truest sense of that word: Mohammed was duped by the greatest swindler of all time, the Devil. Today, throughout the globe, Satan tries to silence all who are critical of the Koran (al-Qur'an). Satan is afraid that the light of the gospel of Jesus Christ will penetrate the darkness of Islam, exposing him and his lies for what they really are. Paradoxically, it is Satan who is terrorized by that possibility. For this reason, Satan does not want people to read and comprehend the salvation message in the Holy Bible.

Debating Muslims about the Only-Begotten Son of Yahweh

μονογενής (pronounced mo-no-ge-nase´) [G3439] is the most important word in the Greek New Testament when it is used in conjunction with the physical conception and birth of Christ Jesus as the Son of Yahweh, the God of the Holy Bible. μονογενής (mo-no-ge-nase´) is a compound word composed of the two base, or root, words μόνος (pronounced mo-nos´) [G3441] and γεννάω (pronounced gen-au´) [G1080]. μόνος (mo-nos´) means: *one, only, only one, one and only, solitary,* and *unique;* and γεννάω (gen-au´) means: *born* (i.e., delivered from a uterus), *begat, begotten, birthed, conceived, generated,* and *legitimate.*

Because μονογενής (mo-no-ge-nase´) is a compound word, its complete meaning includes the individual meanings of both root words and not just the meaning of one of them. In other words, the full definition for μονογενής (mo-no-ge-nase´) includes: *only-begotten, one and only physically born, only legitimate, uniquely-conceived,* and *solitarily-generated.* Although some Bible scholars have chosen to define μονογενής (mo-no-ge-nase´) by the single word *only* because they believe that the *begotten* portion is redundant, implied, archaic, and/or unrelatable to the modern ear, the definition *only* without *begotten* is, in fact, an undertranslation because it is missing one-half of its full meaning. To be sure, using the single word *only* to define μονογενής (mo-no-ge-nase´) does not impart the same meaning as using *only-begotten*.

Many people do not grasp the meaning of *begotten* in the expression *only-begotten Son of God*. Therefore, for the sake of clarity, it is important to state here that "begotten" is derived from Old English and is the past participle of the verb "beget," whose past tense is "begat" *(beget, begat, begotten)*. The word *beget* means "to bear" *(bear, bore, born)*, "to give birth to," and "to produce offspring." Thus, the word "begotten" means "born," "birthed," "conceived," or "physically delivered from a uterus." The first man Adam was not "begotten" by the God of the Holy Bible because the first man Adam was neither conceived from a fertilized egg nor delivered from a uterus and because the first man Adam was neither self-existent nor equivalent to the Creator-God. Christ Jesus, however, is self-existent and equivalent to the Creator-God *(John 1:1)*. Only Christ Jesus was "the begotten" of God. Although the first man Adam was "the Son of God" (Luke 3:38), the first man Adam was a created being and never God-in-flesh as was Christ Jesus (John 1:14 KJV). (For the sake of clarity, *God-in-flesh* and *God Incarnate* are synonymous.)

In the case of Christ Jesus, "begat by God" and "begotten by God" mean: (1) that God Himself provided the seed and Mary (Miriam) herself provided the egg for the conception of Christ Jesus; (2) that Christ Jesus was physically delivered from Mary's uterus; and (3) that Christ Jesus was composed of the same spiritual substance as God in addition to human flesh. Christ Jesus was not generated through sexual relations but through the Creator-God's Holy Spirit *overshadowing* Mary (Luke 1:35 KJV). Mary the mother was a full participant in the conception and birth of Christ Jesus through her personal physical contributions of egg, uterus, and placental nutrition. Mary was not just an incubator into which a second created Adam had been placed. Although Yahweh is the Father and Mary is the mother of Christ Jesus, and Christ Jesus is God-in-flesh, Mary is neither *the wife of God* nor *the mother of God*. Christ Jesus was the unique hybrid of the Creator-God's Holy Spirit and Mary's corporeality (i.e., her physical substance).

Although the first man Adam was *created* in the complete image and perfect likeness of the Creator-God, the first man Adam was not equal to the Creator-God. In other words, the first man Adam was not God. In contrast, Christ Jesus was composed of the same self-existent substance as God and, as such, is uniquely one in *being* with the Creator-God. In other words, Christ Jesus was, is, and always will be the same as God because he, in fact, is God Himself. The first man Adam was made only of *created* substance; in contrast, Christ Jesus was composed of the same self-existent substance as God, who uniquely appeared in flesh. (Christ Jesus was, is, and always will be God regardless of the state or condition of being that his personhood was, is, or will be in.)

In order to define *only-begotten* correctly concerning Christ Jesus, it is important to properly contextualize μονογενής (mo-no-ge-nase´) according to the writings of John the Apostle. Christ Jesus is known as "the Word of God" not only in Revelation 19:13 (written by John the Apostle) but also in the Gospel According to John:

> {1} In the beginning was the Word, and the Word was with God, and the Word was God. {2} The same was in the beginning with God. {3} All things were made by him; and without him was not anything made that was made. {4} In him was life; and the life was the light of all people. {5} And the life's light had shone in darkness, but darkness could not comprehend it. {10} He was in the world, and the world was made by him, but the world did not recognize who he was. {14} And the Word was made flesh, and dwelt among us, and we beheld his glory — the glory as of the only begotten [μονογενής] of the Father, full of grace and truth. {18} No one has seen God at any time; the only begotten [μονογενής] Son, who is at the core of the Father, he has declared Him. {34} And I [John] saw him, and bare record that he is the Son of God. {49} And Nathanael responded to Jesus and said, "Rabbi, you are the Son of God; you are the King of Israel."
>
> *John 1:1-5, 10, 14, 18, 34, & 49 KJV (Paraphrase)*

To summarize at this juncture:

1. Christ Jesus is "the *Word* of God" (Revelation 19:13 KJV).

2. The *Word* of God is the Creator-God (John 1:1 KJV).

3. The *Word* was made flesh as the only-begotten Son of God in Christ Jesus (John 1:14, 18, 34, and 35 KJV).

4. Christ Jesus is *God Incarnate* (i.e., God-in-flesh).

5. The Creator-God was in the world that he had made, but the world did not recognize him because those in darkness could not see his transfigured glory — the glory that John, James, and Peter had witnessed on the mountain when Christ Jesus spoke with Elijah and Moses (John 1:4, 5, 10, and 14 KJV).

Because of his unique conception as the *only-begotten* Son of God, Christ Jesus is fully God and fully man. No one else can ever lay claim — or will ever be able to lay claim — to that singular status.

The Koran (al-Qur'an) is quite clear that who it purports to be the Creator (i.e., *Allah*) does not have an *only-begotten* Son in Christ Jesus (see quotations from the Koran associated with Endnotes numbered 18 through 29 in this chapter). However, some literate Muslims concede that Christ Jesus *is* the Son of God but only to the same degree that other people in the Bible are referred to as Sons of God. Three important examples follow:

Example One

(1) First, some literate Muslims believe that Christ Jesus as the Son of God is no different from Adam because Adam is clearly referred to as "the Son of God" in Luke 3:38 (KJV).

However, in response to the argument that Adam was the Son of God, it is important to note that Adam was not *begotten* by God: Adam was created out of unformed matter, or *dust* (Genesis 2:7). Adam was not born of a human mother. Christ Jesus is the only *begotten* Son of God. That means that Christ Jesus is the only Son of God who was begotten by God's Holy Spirit in consort with a human female. The God of the Holy Bible was the Father and Mary was the mother of Christ Jesus. Both God the Father and Mary the mother were equal physical contributors to the birth of Christ Jesus: Christ Jesus was begotten from a materialized seed (i.e., spermatozoon) provided by God the Father and from a physical egg (i.e., oocyte) provided by Mary the mother. Although the spermatozoon may have been materialized: (1) out of unformed matter (i.e., *de novo*), (2) out of *chaos* (i.e., *ex nihilo*), or (3) out of deific genetic manipulation, the egg alone was provided by Mary. Christ Jesus was not conceived by some strange form of spontaneous generation within Mary's womb. Christ Jesus was not conceived without Mary's haploid chromosomal contribution. Christ Jesus was not cloned from Mary.

Because Mohammed's understanding of Christianity came from his superficial exposure to Roman Catholicism, Eastern Orthodoxy, and Coptic (i.e., Egyptian) Christianity, Mohammed did not fully comprehend the concept of the three parts of the Godhead (i.e., God the Father, God the Son, and God the Holy Spirit). Because of the pagan idolatry of Mary that existed, and still exists, in Roman Catholicism, Eastern Orthodoxy, and Coptic Christianity, Mohammed erroneously concluded that Mary was considered by Christians to be the third part of the tri-unity of the God of the Holy Bible as "God the Mother" in addition to God the Father and God the Son. Mohammed's attempt to portray Mary as the third part of the tri-unity of the Christian God is made in the first half of verse 116 of Surah V (al-Ma'idah):

> And when [Allah] said, "O Jesus son of Mary, didst thou say unto men, 'Take me and my mother as gods apart from [Allah]?'"
>
> *Surah 5.116* [60]

For the sake of clarification, regardless of the Mariolatry (i.e., pagan idolatry of Mary) that exists in Roman Catholicism, Eastern Orthodoxy, and Coptic Christianity, Mary is not considered to be "God the Mother" or the third part of the tri-unity of God anywhere in mainstream Christianity, not even in the three sects of Christianity just mentioned. All authentic Christians know that Mary was a human being, not the wife of God, and certainly was never part of the Godhead. Mohammed did not comprehend this. (Although Mohammed did not comprehend it, Satan did comprehend it and, as a result, designed the Koran (al-Qur'an) to confuse Muslims and prospective Muslims by obfuscating the truth about Mary's status and role in the conception of Christ Jesus.)

Example Two

(2) Second, some literate Muslims also believe that Christ Jesus as the *begotten* Son of God is no different from King David because they have erroneously concluded that King David was referred to as a *begotten* Son of God in Psalm 2:7:

> {6} Yet have I set My king upon My holy hill of Zion. {7} I will declare the decree: the LORD has said unto me, "You are My Son; this day have I begotten you. {8} Ask of Me, and I will give you the heathen for your inheritance, and the uttermost parts of the earth for your possession. {9} You shall break them with a rod of iron; you will dash them into pieces like a potter's vessel."
> *Psalm 2:6-9 KJV (Paraphrase)*

Muslims who think that Psalm 2 is referring to King David are mistaken. They don't understand that Psalm 2 is prophetic Scripture about the *King of kings* (i.e., the Messiah) and not about King David. In other words, the King referenced in Psalm 2:6 is Christ Jesus, and the "begotten Son" referenced in Psalm 2:7 is Christ Jesus, not King David. The Lord God Almighty clearly states in Psalm 2:8: "Ask Me, and I will give you the heathen for your inheritance, and the uttermost parts of the earth for your possession." The Hebrew word for "the heathen" (or "the nations" in other Bible translations) is "goyim" [H1471], which means "the Gentiles." King David did not rule over the Gentiles throughout the whole world (i.e., to "the uttermost parts of the earth"): King David was the king over the children of Israel in the Holy Land. Only the Savior of the world, Christ Jesus, rules over Gentiles throughout the whole world. Psalm 2:9 confirms that the entire second psalm is about the Savior by referencing his rule of the whole world with "a rod of iron" (see Revelation 12:5 and 19:15). To further confirm this understanding, whenever the *begotten* from Psalm 2:7 is referenced in the New Testament (Acts 13:33, Hebrews 1:5, and Hebrews 5:5), it is *always* concerning Christ Jesus and not King David.

Example Three

(3) Third, some literate Muslims point to various verses in the Holy Bible to prove that there are other "Sons of God" besides Jesus Christ:

…the sons of God saw that the daughters of men were attractive, and they made wives of all that they chose.
Genesis 6:2 KJV (Paraphrase)

Muslims do not understand that the phrase "sons of God" here refers to angelic beings who left their first estate in Heaven to have sexual intercourse with human beings (see verse 6 of Jude). They also fail to understand that the phrase "sons of God" used in the New Testament (John 1:12; Romans 8:14 and 19; Philippians 2:15; and 1 John 3:1 and 2) refers to people who are "heirs" of Christ Jesus (or "co-heirs" with him) through their faith in his atoning sacrifice.

A word to the wise for those of you who would debate Muslims about the Son of God:

Some of you might enter into a debate with Muslims without recognizing that you are being baited by people who think they know everything. Please understand that, in most cases, you will not succeed in changing their minds. Unfortunately, your debate with them will end up as a frustrating intellectual exercise. The questions that are asked by most literate Muslims are very strategic and posed in the hopes of getting you to accede to at least one doctrinal point in their belief system so that they might (1) eventually win you over to their entire way of thinking or (2) embarrass you in front of non-Christian believers to make you a less effective witness.

If you just want to sharpen your debating skills (i.e., forensic skills) and increase your abilities in Christian apologetics, those are good enough reasons to engage in debate with Muslims. However, don't remain naive concerning: (1) the unwillingness of Muslims to learn about the true nature of Christ Jesus; and (2) the probable outcome of your time, effort, and energy.

In order to be saved, people can't just believe that Christ Jesus existed. People must believe that Christ Jesus is the *only-begotten* Son of God and accept him as their personal Savior. That is why the "blasphemies" written about in Revelation 13 (see the Fifth Chapter in this book) are about blaspheming the God of the Holy Bible by telling Him that He cannot have an *only-begotten* Son. The Wrath of the God of the Holy Bible rests on those who tell Him that He cannot have an *only-begotten* Son and on those who tell Him that Christ Jesus is not His *only-begotten* Son.

> {35} The Father loves the Son [Christ Jesus] and has given all things into his hand. {36} He who believes in the Son [Christ Jesus] has eternal life; but he who does not obey the Son [Christ Jesus] will not see life [in heaven], but the wrath of God abides on him. [brackets mine]
>
> *John 3:35-36 KJV*

For as long as people on Earth consciously reject Christ Jesus as the *only-begotten* Son of Yahweh and God Incarnate, they place themselves under the curse of Yahweh's Wrath (i.e., His Justified Anger) not only while they are on Earth but also throughout eternity. However, for the duration that souls are in corporeality (i.e., in a human body), they still have an opportunity (not necessarily just *one* opportunity) to remove themselves from the curse of Yahweh by: (1) accepting Christ Jesus as the *only-begotten* Son of Yahweh and God-in-flesh; and (2) accepting his sacrifice on the cross of Calvary as the only sacrifice acceptable to God the Father for the atonement of their iniquity and sins and the remission of the debt they owe for their iniquity and sins.

Satan and his demons do not mind if people accept that: (1) Christ Jesus is one prophet of many prophets; (2) Christ Jesus was born of a virgin (Mary); (3) Christ Jesus is the prophesied Messiah of Israel; (4) Christ Jesus was a worker of miracles; and (5) Christ Jesus will return one day to defeat the Antichrist, or False Messiah (i.e., *al-Masih ad-Dajjal*). However, Satan and his demons are adamant that no one on Earth learn that: (1) Christ Jesus is the *only-begotten* Son of God; (2) Christ Jesus is the only incarnation of God in flesh; (3) Christ Jesus is the Savior of the world; and (4) Christ Jesus is our personal Savior — all four concepts both explicitly and implicitly stated and restated in the New Testament.

By influencing human beings to reject the four concepts given in the previous paragraph, Satan helps confirm for Christians that, of all theological concepts, these four concepts are the most powerful for people on Earth to know. Why are they the most powerful? They threaten Satan in his mission to prevent the salvation of human beings and, thereby, rob Yahweh of the restoration of His fallen creation. To be sure, although Satan is the enemy of all human beings, Satan is only our indirect enemy; Satan's true Enemy is Yahweh, the God of the Holy Bible. It is for this reason that Satan seeks to rob Yahweh of His creation. Satan erroneously believes that, by robbing Yahweh of His creation, Satan will unseat Yahweh as Supreme Being and replace Him as universal Sovereign.

Everything that Satan has done after his fall has been to fulfill his desire of robbing the Creator-God, Yahweh, of His creation, unseat the Creator-God as Supreme Being, and replace the Creator-God as universal Sovereign. To this end, throughout history Satan has tried to: (1) murder all Jews, (2) murder all Christians, (3) discredit the witness of Jews and Christians, (4) firmly establish the Antichrist religion of Islam throughout the Earth, and (5) cause all people on Earth to doubt the accuracy of the Old and New Testaments and the validity of the gospel message of salvation through Christ Jesus alone as the *only-begotten* Son of God and God-in-flesh.

In transitioning to the next chapter, it is important for the reader to always remember that Christ Jesus is God Incarnate. *That* is why Christ Jesus is worshiped. Christ Jesus said: "I am Alpha and Omega, the beginning and the end, and the First and the Last" (Revelation 22:13 KJV). According to the unified language of the Holy Bible, saying "I am the First and Last" is equivalent to saying "I am God." *For example,* in Isaiah 41:4, the God of the Holy Bible states: "Who has wrought and done it, calling the generations from the beginning? I the LORD, the First, and the Last; I am He." And in Isaiah 44:6, God states: "Thus says the LORD the King of Israel, and his redeemer the LORD of hosts; I am the First, and I am the Last; and beside Me there is no God." Perhaps two of the most difficult concepts for non-Christians to understand about Christ Jesus include: (1) in Christ Jesus, the Creator-God inhabited a created body; and (2) the Creator-God resurrected the physical body of Christ Jesus after it was dead.

CHAPTER FOUR
How It All Adds Up

The Name, Number, and Mark of the Beast

Central to Christianity is the doctrine of eternal salvation through the substitutionary blood atonement of Christ Jesus for the forgiveness of our sins and cancellation of the debt we owe to the God of the Holy Bible for our sins. Certainly, the Lamb of God's sacrifice does not relieve any one of us of our own burdens or responsibilities. Nor does it take away from the Apostle Paul's admonition for us to "work out our own salvation with fear and trembling" (Philippians 2:12 KJV Paraphrase).

What Christ Jesus did was reconcile us to God the Father that we might receive forgiveness (a restoration to fellowship with Him and all who belong to Him) through grace, God's unmerited favor. By resisting temptation all the way to Calvary, Christ Jesus was eternally victorious over the Tempter (i.e., the Devil or Satan). Through the self-sacrificing life that was in him, our Lord Jesus brought spiritual gifts for all who would believe on him. He paved the way for us back to our Creator. To say that Christ Jesus was just a mortal is far from the Truth. To say that Christ Jesus was not the *only-begotten* Son of God is a lie and blasphemy. To say that Christ Jesus did not die for our sins is heresy:

Who is a liar but the person who denies that Jesus is the Christ? He is antichrist that denies the Father and the Son. Whoever denies the Son, the same does not have the Father; but the person that acknowledges the Son has the Father also.
1 John 2:22-23 KJV

Hereby know you the Spirit of God: every spirit that confesses that Jesus Christ is come in the flesh is of God: And every spirit that does not confess that Jesus Christ is come in the flesh is not of God: and this is that spirit of antichrist, whereof you have heard that it should come; and even now already is it in the world.
1 John 4:2-3 KJV

The person who believes on the Son of God has the witness in himself/herself: the person who does not believe God has made God a liar because he/she does not believe the record that God gave of His Son.
1 John 5:10 KJV (Paraphrase)

For many deceivers are entered into the world, who confess not that Jesus Christ is come in the flesh. This is the spirit of a deceiver and an antichrist.
2 John, verse 7 KJV

It should be obvious to the discerning reader that Mohammed has tried to make Christ Jesus' life of null effect for sinners. True, Mohammed has been just one of many who have tried to discredit the *only-begotten* Son of God. However, Mohammed is not just one antichrist of many antichrists: Bible prophecy reveals his testimony as testimony of *the* end-time Antichrist.

In the Thirteenth Chapter of Revelation, it is written:

> Here is wisdom. Let the person who has understanding count the number of the beast: for it is the number of a man; and his number is Six hundred threescore and six (666).
>
> *Revelation 13:18 KJV*

The beast referred to here is the confederacy of Islamic states that is taking shape during these last days. The man is Mohammed — the identification coming from the ancient Hebrew science that assigns numerical values to individual letters and words. In that science, the value of a word is determined by adding the numerical equivalents of the individual letters that form it.

Table One on the next page shows the five major steps necessary for identifying Mohammed as the "name" and "number" of the beast in Revelation 13:18. In summary, understanding the cryptographic rendering of "666" depends on using a transposition cipher (i.e., a transposition code or encryption) that combines a backward cipher (in this case, writing in reverse order the characters in the Hebrew word for *Mohammed)* with (1) a numeric substitution cipher (in this case, substituting numbers for the characters used in the reversed Hebrew word for *Mohammed)* and (2) a mathematic cipher (in this case, adding the substituted numbers in the reversed Hebrew word for *Mohammed,* which total "666").

Please also refer to Appendix A in this book for additional details and clarifications concerning the characters and numerical values associated with the reverse order cryptographic transliteration shown on the following page in Table One.

The simplest phonetic transcription of "Mohammed" is:

(1) M O H A M E D

In ancient Hebrew, the closest counterparts of these sounds are:

(2) Mem Waw Hey Aleph Mem Yod Dalet

The proper character representation for "Mohammed" in John's vision is:

(3) ם ו ה א מ י ד

Note: The Apostle John thought, understood, and "saw" in Hebrew, which is written from right to left. However, the backward cipher transcribes this Hebrew word from left to right. Thus, the so-called "final Mem" (the representation of Mem when it ends a Hebrew word) is used in the beginning place here.

In Hebrew, the numerical equivalents of the characters above are, respectively:

(4) 600 6 5 1 40 10 4

(5) The sum of the above numbers is 666, or "Six hundred threescore and six" (Revelation 13:18 KJV).

Copyright 1981 by Rev. Joseph Adam Pearson, Ph.D.
TXu000075639 United States Copyright Office
Author email: drjosephadampearson@gmail.com

Table One

When you stop to think about it, everything fits: (1) That "the fourth beast shall be the fourth kingdom upon earth, which shall be diverse from all kingdoms, and shall devour the whole earth, and shall tread it down, and break it into pieces" (Daniel 7:23 KJV): The nation of Islam, with all of its oil-rich countries, will wield more power than any earthly kingdom previously known. (2) That an end-time ruler shall "think to change times" (Daniel 7:25 KJV): The Muslim era, or Islamic Calendar, dates from the Hegira, the forced journey of Mohammed from Mecca to Medina in 622 A.D. (3) That the final end-time ruler shall not regard "the desire of women" (Daniel 11:37 KJV): Sharia, or Islamic Law, presents women as being little better than livestock and the property of men. And (4) that men shall have "the name of the beast" (Revelation 13:17 KJV): Today, the word "Mohammed" is the most popularly used name in the world. People have incorporated "Mohammed" and its variations and derivations *(for example, Mahmoud, Mehmet,* and *Ahmed)* into their names more than any other word.

What is the ultimate fate of latter-day Muslims who continue to proclaim that Jesus Christ is *not* the *only-begotten* Son of God? Their fate is described in Revelation 14:9-11:

> {9} If any person worships the beast and his image, and receives his mark in his forehead or in his hand, {10} the same shall drink of the wine of the wrath of God, which is poured out without mixture into the cup of His indignation; and that person shall be tormented with fire and brimstone in the presence of the holy angels, and in the presence of the Lamb: {11} And the smoke of their torment ascends up forever and ever: and they have no rest day nor night, who worship the beast and his image, and whosoever receives the mark of his name.
>
> *Revelation 14:9-11 KJV*

For the sake of clarity, the "mark in the forehead" figuratively represents worshiping the god of Islam and the "mark in the hand" figuratively represents working directly or indirectly on behalf of the god of Islam. The figurative language of "forehead" and "hand" reminds us of these two general types of commitment (i.e., worship and service) in the wearing of the tefillin (singular *tefilah*) that God required of the Jews as recorded in the Old Testament:

> Therefore shall you lay up these my words in your heart and in your soul, and bind them for a sign upon your hand, [and] that they may be as forehead adornments between your eyes. [brackets mine]
> *Deuteronomy 11:18 KJV*

The forehead tefilah represents: (1) remembering God, (2) communicating with God, and (3) worshiping God. The hand tefilah represents working for God, or doing the work of God. Thus, for Jews, the forehead and the hand are the two sites where they are to bind the tefillin, or phylacteries, which contain at least the following two verses from the Sixth Chapter of the Book of Deuteronomy:

> {4} Hear, O Israel: the LORD our God, the LORD, is one. {5} And you shall love the LORD your God with all your heart, and with all your soul, and with all your might.
> *Deuteronomy 6:4-5 KJV*

Whomever or whatever we worship, we eventually become. In other words, whom or what we worship gradually becomes our sole identity. If we worship "the god of this world" (i.e., Satan) long enough (2 Corinthians 4:4 KJV), then our identity is forever lost and entangled in the identity of that god. If we worship the Lord God Almighty with all of our heart, soul, mind, and strength, then our identity is completely, fully, perfectly, and eternally immersed in Him.

We become whomever or whatever we worship because we are fused to whom or what we worship and are infused by the essence of that identity as well. Of course, we do not become God, but He does infuse us with Himself through His Holy Spirit. Rather than proclaim that Jesus Christ is our first priority because we worship him and him alone, in the reality of God there is no such thing as priority when every aspect of our being is permeated with and by Jesus Christ.

The figurative interpretation of "forehead" and "hand" does not preclude the existence of additional marks, signs, and symbols such as: required stamped insignias, membership or identification cards, work permits and visas, pass booklets, tattoos, digital encodings, subcutaneous microchips, visible body piercings, fingerprinting, scans of the eye's iris and retinal vasculature, and written or spoken declarations of allegiance to Allah, Islam, and the so-called "Seal of the Prophets" (Mohammed).

Current examples of marks, signs, and symbols of dedication and sacrifice to the god of Islam include the combined star and crescent as well as the Arabic stamp for *halal:*

Representative Symbols for the Beast

Figure One

Meat with the halal symbol means that it has been prepared according to Islamic Law and, therefore, dedicated or sacrificed to the false god *Allah* by Muslim butchers who slaughter livestock. Many butchers throughout the world are Muslim and dedicate the slaughter of their animals to the false god *Allah* before they sell meat to local people or ship meat to other places for sale. They often do so by proclaiming *Bismillah* (i.e., "in the name of Allah") one time and *Allahu Akbar* (i.e., "*Allah* is the greater/greatest [god]") three times as part of the sacrificial rite. In this way, unknown to them, many Jews and Christians eat meat sacrificed to an idol — in particular, the false god called *Allah*. (One can have an idol without an actual statue, figure, figurine, or icon.)

With regard to Christians eating food sacrificed to idols, the most important point to make here is that some decisions in Christianity are a matter of conscience. *For example:* (1) Christians get to decide if they are willing to fight in a war or not. (2) Christians get to decide to drink an alcoholic beverage or not. (3) Christians get to decide if they are willing to kill someone to protect their families or not. And (4) Christians get to decide if they are willing to eat food sacrificed to idols or not. However, our Creator-God wants us to carefully consider options and make choices for ourselves that are defensible as well as pleasing to Him.

The present author does not want to take away anyone's ability to make a choice for himself or herself. However, the following things should be said about Christians eating food sacrificed to idols: (1) The Apostle Paul stated: "Be careful that the exercise of your rights does not become a stumbling block to those who are weak" (1 Corinthians 8:9 KJV Paraphrase). In other words, Christians should not try to negatively influence others or tempt them to do things with which they might feel uncomfortable. (2) Acts 15:28-29 (KJV Paraphrase) states: "For it seems good to the Holy Spirit and to us to lay upon you no greater burden than the following requirements: That you abstain from eating meat offered to idols, from eating blood, from eating strangled animals, and from sex outside of marriage. If you keep yourselves from doing these things, you will be doing well."

The two verses just quoted from Acts were written at a time when Jewish Christians were still struggling with what would be required of Gentiles when they became Christians. Some Jewish Christians wanted all Gentile males to be circumcised as well as follow all dietary and hygiene rules from the Book of Leviticus in the Old Testament. However, in order to not deter Gentiles from becoming Christians, the Jewish Christians decided on a simple list of things that Gentile Christians should not do in order that Jewish non-Christians not be influenced negatively by the actions of Gentile Christians. *For example,* Gentile Christians were advised not to eat meat sacrificed to idols because Jewish non-Christians would find it barbaric and pagan and, as a result, might not be willing to convert to Christianity or accept Gentile Christians.

In the final analysis, concerning eating meat sacrificed to idols (including the false god Allah), everyone must decide what to do for himself or herself. Anyone who tells you that you must do one thing or another with regard to this matter is trying to control you by attempting to rob you of the individual free will that our Creator-God has given to each person.

The Named God versus the Unnamed Counterfeit

Calling the god of Islam "Allah" — which means "the god" — does not identify by name who the god referenced in the Koran (al-Qur'an) really is. Just because Jews and Christians may also call the Creator "God," "Theos," "Deus," "El," or "Eloah" does not mean that they do not know the Name of the God of the Holy Bible. The God of Jews and Christians identified Himself by name to Moses (Moshe) when Moses asked Him: "Who shall I say sent me?"

When asked for His name by Moses, God replied: "I AM THAT I AM," or EYEH ASHER EYEH [H1961] [H834] [H1961], and "Tell the children of Israel that "I AM," or EYEH [H1961], has sent you" (Exodus 3:14). Regardless of how it is pronounced, the most holy Biblical name of God is YHWH [H3068] (often pronounced *Yahweh, Yehowah,* or *Yehovah);* and YHWH [H3068] is derived from EYEH [H1961]. The name YHWH is so holy to Jews that, instead of pronouncing it, they will either (1) substitute *Adonai* (i.e., "Lord") instead of reading it out loud or (2) substitute *H'Shem* (i.e., "the Name") when in conversation. (Details for the original Hebrew and Greek words indicated by numbers in brackets are provided in Table Two of this chapter.)

The *I AM* identity for the God of the Holy Bible is echoed by Christ Jesus when he answered the Jews who questioned his authority. Christ Jesus said: "Before Abraham was, I AM" (John 8:58). Through his response, Christ Jesus clearly proclaimed himself to be one with the Lord God Almighty. Jesus did not say: "Before Abraham, I was" — which is to say, "I existed before Abraham" (although he clearly did). Rather, Christ Jesus was conveying that he exists in an eternal state of being in the Godhead and that "God the Son" is fully, completely, and perfectly one with "God the Father."

Jesus Christ, Christ Jesus, Jesus the Christ, and *Y'shua H'Moshiach* are all synonymous names for the only Messiah of Israel and one true Savior of the world.

To use the word *Jesus* alone when referring to the Savior is insufficient because there are ordinary mortals who possess the same name. Y'shua (Jeshua) [H3442] is derived from Yehoshuah (Jehoshua) [H3091] — of which: (1) "Iesous" [G2424] is the Ionic Greek form; (2) "Iesus" [IESVS] is the Classical Latin form; and (3) "Jesus" is the Early Modern English form. The Hebrew name Yehoshuah [H3091] means "YAH (or EYEH) is our salvation" — which is to say, "*the Self-Existent One,* or the Great *I AM,* is our salvation." (Details for the original Hebrew and Greek words indicated by numbers in brackets are provided in Table Two of this chapter.)

To use the name *Christ* alone when referring to the Savior is insufficient because, when used alone, although it can accurately imply a spiritual state of mind and a heightened level of consciousness, it can also inaccurately imply that the spiritual state of mind and heightened level of consciousness may be achieved without accepting the Biblical Jesus as (1) the *only-begotten* Son of God, (2) the only Messiah of Israel, and (3) the one true Savior of the world. Indeed, one cannot have "the Christ," "the mind of Christ," "divine Mind," or "Christ Consciousness" without accepting the shed blood of the *only-begotten* Son of God as the only sacrifice acceptable to God the Father for the remission of our sins (i.e., the cancellation of the debt we owe to Him for our sins). To be sure, the crucifixion, or blood sacrifice, of Christ Jesus provides the only acceptable substitutionary atonement for our sins.

One cannot have "Jesus" without having "the Christ" and one cannot have "the Christ" without having "Jesus." Christians should always hold the whole name, "Jesus the Christ," while they simultaneously attend to its two parts: "Jesus" and "the Christ." The words *Jesus* and *Christ* are inextricably linked together and should rarely be used separately so as not to confuse the hearer, the reader, or even oneself (yes, we can easily confuse ourselves). The English word *Christ* is a title derived from the Greek word *Christos* [G5547] and its counterpart in Latin, *Christus* [CHRISTVS]. The Greek word *Christos* [G5547] is a translation of the Hebrew word *H'Moshiach* [H4899], which means "*the* Messiah" or "*the* Anointed One" in English. And the Greek word *Messias* [G3323] is the transliterated form of the Hebrew word *Moshiach* [H4899]. (Details for the original Hebrew and Greek words indicated by numbers in brackets are provided in Table Two of this chapter.)

That both *God the Father* and *God the Son* have the same identity ("I AM") does not mean that they have the same personality or the same function in the universe even though they both have the same purpose and are co-equal parts of the triune Godhead along with *God the Holy Spirit.* Jesus the Christ said: "I and my Father are one" (John 10:30 KJV). To be sure, God the Father and God the Son are one, and they have the same identity ("I AM"), but they also have *Self*-assigned functions that are different from each other.

In the last sentence of the previous paragraph, I have capitalized the word *Self* to distinguish it as the sole identity of the Godhead, consisting of God the Father, God the Son, and God the Holy Spirit — the equivalent, consubstantial, and triadic elements of the one true and only real Supreme Being, Creator, and Lord of the Universe. (God the Father, God the Son, and God the Holy Spirit all possess the same *Being*.)

In order to understand the nature of the Godhead more fully, it might be helpful for you to read these three books that I have written: (1) *As I See It: The Nature of Reality by God* (ISBN 978-0615590615); (2) *God, Our Universal Self: A Primer for Future Christian Metaphysics* (ISBN 978-0985772857); and (3) *Divine Metaphysics of Human Anatomy* (ISBN 978-0985772819) — all of which detail who God is and why God originally partitioned Himself into a triadic state. (Go to www.christevangelicalbibleinstiute.com to get free pdf files and free mobi files of these three books.) That "God the Father" and "God the Son" are one does not make them the same nor does it make them sequential manifestations of the Godhead to humanity. *God the Son* did not replace *God the Father*. And *God the Holy Spirit* did not replace *God the Son*.

Some denominational Christians go to an extreme when they interpret "the Lord God is *one* Lord" (Deuteronomy 6:4 KJV) to mean that "God the Father" *is* "God the Son." Although Jesus Christ is: (a) the *only-begotten* Son of God (John 3:16; Matthew 16:16); (b) God Incarnate (Colossians 2:9; 1 Timothy 3:16); and (c) one with God the Father (John 17:11), Jesus Christ *is not* God the Father. Although the two are one, they are not the same.

Strong's Number	Hebrew or Greek Word	Transliteration in Syllables	English Equivalents and Definitions
H188	אוֹי	ō′·ē	1. woe 2. (cry of) lamentation
H834	אֲשֶׁר	ash·er′	1. that 2. which 3. who
H1961	אֶהְיֶה	eh·yeh′ (ä·yä′)	1. I am 2. I become (I will be) 3. I exist
H3068	יְהוָה	Yeh·hō·vä′ (Yah·weh′)	1. the Existing One 2. the Self-Existing One 3. the Self-Existent One
H3091	יְהוֹשׁוּעַ	Yeh·hō·shü′·ah	1. Yehoshua or Jehoshua 2. Yoshua or Joshua 3. Yeshua or Jeshua 4. Y'shua or Yashua
H3442	יֵשׁוּעַ	Ye·shü′·ah	1. Yeshua or Jeshua 2. Y'shua or Yashua 3. Yesus or Jesus
H4899	מָשִׁיחַ	mä·shē′·akh	1. Moshiach 2. Messiah 3. Anointed One
H4899 with definite article	הַמָּשִׁיחַ	hä·mä·shē′·akh	1. H'Moshiach 2. the Moshiach 3. the Messiah 4. the Anointed One
G2424	Ἰησοῦς	E·ā·sü′·s	1. Iesous 2. Jesus 3. Yesus
G3323	Μεσσίας	Mes·sē′·äs	1. Messias 2. Messiah 3. Anointed One
G5547	Χριστός	Khrē·stos′	1. Christ 2. Messiah 3. Anointed One

Table Two

The theological position that *God the Son* replaced *God the Father* is untenable because it is unable to offer plausible explanations concerning: (1) the synchronous, or simultaneous, presence of *God the Father* and *God the Son* at the times when *God the Father* proclaimed: "This is My beloved Son in whom I am well pleased" (Matthew 3:17 KJV; 17:5 KJV); (2) to whom Jesus Christ was speaking from the cross when he said: "Father, forgive them for they do not know what they do" (Luke 23:34 KJV); and (3) to whom Jesus Christ will deliver the Kingdom after *all* enemies of God have been finally conquered:

> And when all things shall be subdued unto him *[God the Son]*, then shall the Son also himself be subject unto him *[God the Father]* that put all things under him *[God the Son]*, that God *[the Father]* may be all in all. [brackets mine]
> 1 Corinthians 15:28 KJV

Jesus Christ is "the Word" and "the Word was, and is, God" (see John 1:1-5), but Jesus Christ is not *God the Father*. The roles of *God the Father* and *God the Son* are different although the Father and the Son are one in the Godhead — along with the Holy Spirit — and all three serve the same Self-existent purpose.

To be sure, Christ Jesus ("God the Son") already has all authority and all power in Heaven and on Earth (Matthew 28:27 and Ephesians 1:22), but not every enemy has been finally conquered yet, or "subdued unto him" (1 Corinthians 15:28 KJV). *For example,* the end-time Antichrist has not yet been overcome. And death, or mortality, itself remains to be conquered. Scripture teaches that the Antichrist will be thrown into the Lake of Fire at the time of Christ Jesus' return to Earth (Revelation 19:20). Scripture also teaches that death, or mortality, is the final enemy that must and will be conquered (1 Corinthians 15:26) when, at the end of the coming Millennium of Peace, it — along with Hades (the current holding tank for unsaved souls) — will be thrown into the Lake of Fire at the time of the Great White Throne Judgment (Revelation 20:11-14), during which Judgment each remaining soul will either be assigned eternal salvation or eternal damnation.

The God of Jews and Christians has a specific name, found in God's response to Moses and in the specific name of *Jesus* for the Christ (i.e., the Messiah). In contrast, the god of Muslims is nameless. The god of Islam refused to name himself in the Koran (al-Qur'an) because he did not want people to know who he really is. If he had said: "I am *the god of this world"* (2 Corinthians 4:4 KJV), or "I am *the prince of the power of the air"* (Ephesians 2:2 KJV), people would not have embraced him to the extent and to the degree that they have. Of course, the god of Islam identifies himself in the foundational literature that he produced. How? The Koran (al-Qur'an) specifically states multiple times: (1) that *Allah* has no *only-begotten* Son, (2) that *Allah* does not need to have an *only-begotten* Son, (3) that Jesus Christ was only a human messenger, and (4) that Jesus Christ was not crucified in the flesh. Therefore, the god of Muslims is *not* the God of Jews and Christians nor is the god of the Koran (al-Qur'an) the same as the God of the Holy Bible. The God of the Holy Bible has an *only-begotten* Son. *Allah,* the god of the Koran (al-Qur'an), does not.

Indeed, neither is the fallen Angel "Lucifer" the same as the Archangel "Gabriel." It was the fallen Angel Lucifer who dictated the Koran (al-Qur'an) to Mohammed, not the Archangel Gabriel — as Mohammed erroneously believed and claimed. Mohammed was duped by Lucifer into believing that he (i.e., Lucifer) was Gabriel. All Mohammed really knew was that an invisible messenger regularly spoke to him. To be sure, the Holy Bible clarifies that Satan is able to falsely present himself as a heavenly angel (2 Corinthians 11:14 KJV).

Although some people, including some Jews and Christians, might see no harm in using the transliterated Arabic word *Allah* for "God" simply because *Allah* means "*the* god" and is etymologically similar to the Hebrew *"El, Eloah,* and *Elohim,"* the word *Allah* should not be used as a name for the God of the Holy Bible. Why? Using the word *Allah* implies that one has bought into (i.e., believes in) at least part of the systematic theology known as Islam and that one endorses both the Koran (al-Qur'an) as well as the false prophet Mohammed as true. Just as the transliterated Hebrew word *Baal* only means "lord" — and, therefore, seems harmless enough — the word *Baal* would not be used in isolation by a Bible-taught Jew or Christian as a name for the God of the Holy Bible because *Baal* is a specific name used for various pagan gods mentioned in the Old Testament. Similarly, the word *Allah* should not be used for the God of the Holy Bible by Jews or Christians. Like *Baal, Allah* is the specific name for a pagan god. Interestingly, just as *Baal* represents a consolidation of multiple city-state pagan deities during Old Testament times (referred to by the plural Hebrew word *Baalim*), so does *Allah* represent a consolidation of multiple pre-Islamic pagan deities. Consolidation or not, the words *Baal* and *Allah* represent false gods — who, in turn, represent Satan himself.

In dictating the Koran (al-Qur'an) to Mohammed, Satan preferred to use the word *Allah* to refer to himself because he did not want to identify himself by name. By using the word *Allah* in their proclamations, Muslims are in fact worshiping a god that is nameless and, therefore, unidentifiable not only to themselves but also to other people as well. They do not realize that they are worshiping Satan, the Enemy of the one true and only real God, the God of the Holy Bible. Although *Allah* may be the name for a counterfeit and faceless god, the identity and face of *Allah* is revealed as Satan by comparing and contrasting what is written in the Koran (al-Qur'an) with what is written in the Holy Bible.

That "there is no god but *Allah*" is a boldfaced lie from the Deceiver (Satan) himself, who is the eternal enemy and adversary of the one true and only real God. *Allah* is the Enemy and Adversary of the God of the Holy Bible.

About Whom Shall We Testify?

Gone is the day when Christian people can refer to the God of the Holy Bible simply as *God* and others would know immediately about whom they were referring. To be sure, in this day and age, when authentic Christian people speak to one another about *God,* they know about whom they are speaking — but not everyone else knows. Nominal Christians do not know. Inauthentic Christians do not know. Secular Christians do not know. And, indeed, non-Christians do not know. Most people in this day and age do not know because: (1) they erroneously disbelieve that the God of the Holy Bible is the one true and only real God; (2) they erroneously believe that people from different world religions worship the same deity referred to as *God;* and/or (3) they automatically assume that, when anyone uses the word *God,* they are speaking about the God of the Holy Bible.

It is especially problematic for Christian people in many countries of the world when they hear or read the expression *Allah.* As stated earlier, because the Arabic expression *Allah* means "*the* god" (or, by implication, "the one true and only real god"), many Christian people misconclude that *Allah* and the God of the Holy Bible are one and the same and, therefore, that it is alright for them to use the expression *Allah* when speaking about the God of the Holy Bible. Even though some Bible translations in languages other than English use *Allah* instead of the word or words for *God* in their respective native languages, it is not alright. Even many Islamists (i.e., Islamacists) know that it is not alright to use the Arabic expression *Allah* to refer to the God of the Holy Bible. *For example,* in 2009, a Malaysian court ruled that non-Muslims cannot use the expression *Allah* because *Allah* is exclusive to Islam.

It is important for authentic Christians from all cultural backgrounds, traditions, denominations, and churches to know that they should refrain from using the expression *Allah* unless they are specifically referring to or discussing the god of the Koran (al-Qur'an) in contrast to the God of the Holy Bible. Just as Elijah boldly opposed the false god *Baal* and upheld the one true and only real God, *Yahweh* (1 Kings 18:1-40), so must authentic Christian people boldly oppose the false god *Allah* in favor of the God of the Holy Bible.

When referring to the God of the Holy Bible, Christians should be clear about whom they are referring. Christian people who speak Arabic, and non-Arabic-speaking Christians who have grown accustomed to using the expression *Allah* for the God of the Holy Bible, should: (1) switch to using the name *Yahweh* (or one of its variants, like *Yehowah* or *Yehovah*); or (2) switch to an Arabic expression for *the Lord Jesus* instead of using the Arabic expression *Allah* (see Table Three on the next page). Christians must always remember that the *only-begotten* Son of God is, indeed, "God Incarnate," or "God in flesh" (John 1:1-5, 14; 1 Timothy 3:16).

All authentic Christians, regardless of native language and local dialect, should change how they express gratitude and praise to the God of the Holy Bible as follows: (1) from *"Praise God!"* or *"Praise Allah!"* to *"Praise Yahweh!"* or *"Praise the Lord Jesus Christ!"* (2) from *"I am grateful to God!"* or *"I am grateful to Allah!"* to *"I am grateful to Yahweh!"* or *"I am grateful to the Lord Jesus Christ!"* and (3) from *"I greet you in the name of God!"* or *"I greet you in the name of Allah!"* to *"I greet you in the Name of Yahweh!"* or *"I greet you in the name of the Lord Jesus Christ!"* To avoid potentially awkward situations when encountering a Muslim who uses the expression *"Allah"* in a personal greeting, Christian people should respond with: (1) *"I greet you in the Name of Yahweh!"* (2) *"I greet you in the Name of the God of the Holy Bible!"* (3) *"I return greetings to you in the name of the Lord Jesus!"* or (4) *"I greet you in the name of Jesus Christ!"*

Arabic Expression	السيد يسوع
Transliteration	al-Saiyid Yesua
Pronunciation	a-say′-yid* yes-oo′-a
English Meaning	the Lord Jesus

> * Although transliterated as *al-Saiyid*, the "l" from "al" is silent before certain consonantal sounds in Arabic, including "-s" and "-z." It should also be noted that one must never confuse the word *Saiyid*, when used with the Savior's name (*Yesua*, *Y'shua*, or *Jesus*), with the honorific name or title used for a descendant of Mohammed. In contradistinction, and for the sake of clarity, when used with *Yesua*, *Y'shua*, or *Jesus*, the title *al-Saiyid* means *the one true and only real Lord* — the only Sovereign to whom all fealty, or allegiance, is owed and to whom all obeisance, or submission, is yielded.

Table Three

When in conversation with a Muslim who expresses thanks or praise to Allah, if a Christian feels the need to say anything at all, then he or she might say: (1) *"All praise to Yahweh!"* (2) *"All praise to the Lord Jesus!"* or (3) *"I give all praise to the Lord Jesus for his every provision, reward, and blessing!"* Finally, Christian people should respond to the spoken expression *"insallah"* or *"inshallah"* (i.e., "if Allah wills") with *"May the Will of the God of the Holy Bible surpass all other will!"*

Although the present author has just provided a few examples of declarations that Christians may use, please feel free to modify the statements according to your situation and circumstance as well as your native language and local dialect. Just remember never to grant credibility, thanksgiving, or honor to the god of al-Qur'an by using the expression *Allah* interchangeably with *the God of the Holy Bible;* and only use the generic word *God* when speaking with other people whom you know as authentic Christians. If ever in doubt, always use the expressions "Yahweh," "Jesus Christ," or "the Lord Jesus" (i.e., *a-say'-yid yes-oo'-a*) in place of the generic word *God* and you will be sure not to inadvertently blaspheme the Holy Name of the one true and only real Creator-God, the God of the Holy Bible. It should also be noted that, because some Messianic Jews (i.e., Christian Jews) may feel uncomfortable using the "unpronounceable" tetragrammaton (YHWH) when speaking, they might use Hebrew words like *Adonai* (i.e., "Lord") or *HaShem* (i.e., "the Name") for *the God of the Holy Bible* and *Y'shua H'Moshiach* (i.e., "Jesus the Messiah") for *God the Son.*

When in the presence of Muslims who prostrate themselves to honor their god, Christians should either (1) excuse themselves or (2) sit or stand quietly and pray to the God of the Holy Bible. In the near future, more Christians will be required to unequivocally state their devotion to the God of the Holy Bible and the Lord Jesus and suffer the consequences of such devotion; however, until that decisive moment comes for each individual Christian, Christians should be cautious, judicious, and circumspect in their interactions with Muslims without blaspheming Yahweh or inadvertently renouncing Christ Jesus by giving honor to the false god known as *Allah* and, at the same time, without unnecessarily placing themselves in harm's way. In the final analysis, what is said or not said is a matter of each person's conscience.

Concerning: (1) taking a stand against Islam, (2) when to take a stand against Islam, and (3) when not to take a stand against Islam, each Christian must decide for himself or herself. The guidance given in the previous sentence comes from Scripture — specifically the Fifth

Chapter of 2 Kings — when Naaman asked the Prophet Elisha if it would be alright for him (i.e., Naaman) to bow to the false god Rimmon when he accompanied the pagan king of Syria to the temple of that god. The Prophet Elisha responded: "Go in peace," implying that the Prophet Elisha would not decide for Naaman and that Naaman would have to decide for himself. The Prophet Elisha knew that he could neither condemn nor condone Naaman's action; he knew that the God of the Holy Bible alone is the real Judge of each and every one of our actions.

After many early Christians chose to deny Christ Jesus in order to avoid being thrown to the lions, some later expressed their desire to be reinstated to the Christian community. It was problematic for early Christians concerning whether they should allow, or not allow, those who denied Christ Jesus in such a set of circumstances to be accepted back into the Christian fold. Regardless of discussion and debate, even in contemporary Christian society it still must be concluded that God alone is the only Judge concerning all matters that are addressed here.

In conclusion, because it is a matter of personal conscience, conviction, and commitment, each person must make decisions for himself or herself and for no one else. And no one is to condemn others for their personal decisions. Why? These matters are between the God of the Holy Bible and each individual. Hopefully, all Christians will mature enough in their faith to be able to conclude that, because they no longer belong to themselves but to the God of the Holy Bible, they will no longer seek to please themselves individually but, instead, seek to please the one true and only real Creator-God, the God of the Holy Bible.

Authentic Christians do not belong to themselves. They do not own themselves. They belong to Christ Jesus. It is Christ Jesus who owns them. We were bought with a price, which price is the shed blood of God's *only-begotten* Son. Consequently, it is no longer we who live but Christ Jesus who lives within us (Galatians 2:20b) through God's indwelling Holy Spirit.

CHAPTER FIVE
Prophecy in View of Islam

The Testimony of Jesus

Although souls are not able to fully comprehend the mysteries of the Lord God Almighty while they are on Earth, they may learn through the fulfillment of His prophecies that He *is* (i.e., that He exists). It is a fact that many who have committed their lives to the God of the Holy Bible first came to believe and trust in Him because they learned that His prophecies had been fulfilled and were being fulfilled. And it is a fact that many of the already faithful have had their faith strengthened because of events revealed through Bible prophecy. In short, we are to "despise not prophecies nor prophesying" (1 Thessalonians 5:20 KJV). For what reasons? (1) "The testimony of Jesus is the spirit of prophecy" (Revelation 19:10 KJV); and (2) "the person that has received his testimony [the testimony of Jesus] has set to his or her seal that God is true" (John 3:33 KJV Paraphrase).

Many situations developing on Earth indicate a quick end to this generation — that is, this Age. I am writing of them now not that the end might be averted but: (1) that others might be influenced toward good, God, to accept and receive the Lord Jesus Christ as the *only-begotten* Son of God and their personal Savior; and (2) that children of God might keep their peace as the raging storm surrounding them seeks to engulf them. Things in this world are going to get much worse. It is my hope that people turn more to the Lord God Almighty before they do get much worse. And it is my hope that people not become embittered by tribulations, persecutions, and hardships and that they give the Lord God Almighty the praise, honor, and glory that He deserves regardless of the circumstances they are in.

So that we not despair when finding ourselves in the midst of darkness and, as a result, come to believe that we have been forsaken by God, it is important for us to understand that the unkindness, disobedience, lawlessness, wickedness, immorality, vulgarity, and selfishness we witness — and will witness to an ever greater degree — is merely the "falling away" (2 Thessalonians 2:3 KJV) that so many of the prophets of God and the apostles of His Christ prophesied was to come to pass just prior to Christ's return.

Concerning the global lack of self-restraint and its relationship to the removal of the current world system, it is important to understand that the Earth will come to complete depravity before Christ Jesus returns to establish his millennial rule on Earth. It is God's Will that seedlings of righteousness not be uprooted with weeds of wickedness. It is also God's Will that the weak be given time to grow strong in Him. Therefore, as the return of Jesus Christ draws nigh, we should expect to see a widening gap, a deepening division, and an increasing distinction between the people who belong to God and the people who have no part in Him. There will be no shades of grey when the Shekinah-glory of God appears. Only spiritual light and darkness will be evident. This accounts for the increasing separation of the sheep (the people who belong to God) from the goats (the people who belong to Satan) during these end-times.

Besides an increasingly sick and sinful mass consciousness, there will be widespread famine and pestilence and great earthquakes and wars during the latter times, as Christ Jesus prophesied (Matthew 24:6-7; Mark 13:7-8; Luke 21:9-11). Our Master told of such events that his followers might be better prepared when those signs of the end come to pass. How so, "better prepared?" While nonbelievers will be surprised and offended and made afraid when such horrible things take place, Christian believers will be strengthened. True believers — even if they themselves are suffering — will be able to view the events as the fulfillment of prophecy and, therefore, as continued proof of the omnipotence, omniscience, and omnipresence of the God of the Holy Bible. And, in that proof, they will rejoice because they will know that their also-promised rest will surely follow.

Few people realize how completely linked the fulfillment of prophecy has been, and is, to proof of God's supreme authority. Consider the Holy Bible. Every book and epistle has some prophetic elements in it, from prophecies concerning the children of Israel to prophecies concerning the First Advent of Jesus Christ (his birth) to prophecies concerning his return (his Second Coming or Second Advent).

Prophecies that have to do with end-time events are called "apocalypses," the word *apocalypse* coming from the Greek ἀποκάλυψις *(apokalypsis)* [G602] — meaning, "disclosure," "unveiling," or "revelation." Apocalyptic writings, then, are reports of divine disclosures or spiritual unveilings concerning those things that will take place before the Day of Judgment.

Apocalyptic writings may be found in many places throughout the Holy Bible. However, the *Revelation* of Christ Jesus to the Apostle John is the greatest of all apocalypses. Why? It is the masterpiece of testimony to human beings that God was and is and ever shall be. It unveils the final horrors that will take place in this world, an understanding of which is necessary for end-time *saints* to keep their faith in the one true and only real God during the tribulations and sorrows that are to come (for the sake of clarity here, all authentic Christians, living or dead, are *saints*).

Yes, the future has been predetermined. For those who may be asking themselves "How can that be?" and "Doesn't that speak of predestination?" — I can only say, in response, that failure is built into the outcome from the start of whatever is attempted outside of God's Will. No matter whether the attempt is to build a religious or political system, a nation, a career, a life, or a world — if the intent is not in keeping with the Will of God, then the action is doomed. (Failure may not be evidenced for seven years, seventy years, or even seven thousand years, but, make no mistake, it will come.) Further, just because this world and its heavens are destined to pass away does not mean that God has determined which souls are eternally redeemed and which souls are eternally damned: Each soul determines that for itself. Although the end, or outcome, of one's intent may be clearly seen in Spirit, every soul chooses for itself the direction in which it travels.

For those who may be inclined, upon learning of the fate of this world, to foolishly conclude that the Creator-God is cruel, I wish to remind them that it is human beings who sin and not God. Had God not withheld His Judgment and Wrath, or Justified Anger, we all would have been wiped out long ago. God has been most merciful to transgressors in that He has given us time to repent, ask for forgiveness for our sins, and accept Jesus Christ as the *only-begotten* Son of God and our personal Savior.

Today, people have forgotten not only to fear the God of the Holy Bible but also *how* to fear Him. Out of the misguided need for political correctness and progressivism (which is to say, trying not to offend people), many modern-day theologians and church leaders teach that fearing the God of the Holy Bible only includes respecting and revering Him. However, true fear of the God of the Holy Bible includes, above all other things, *dreading to offend Him.* For authentic Christians, the fear of the Lord God Almighty should include *both* servile fear and filial fear. In other words, the fear of the Lord God Almighty should include awe of His Power, His Judgment, and His Wrath in order to avoid what He hates. (The God of the Holy Bible hates all evil — especially in the worship of false gods and the murder of people who belong to Him.)

Unfortunately, many authentic Christians have decided for themselves that the God of the Holy Bible cannot be loving and wrathful at the same time. They may not realize that the Vengeance of the God of the Holy Bible relates to His Justice and Judgment. Indeed, although God's Wrath does not fall upon authentic Christians, it does fall upon those who openly blaspheme His Holy Name, reject His *only-begotten* Son, and murder His people. Authentic Christians have only come to avoid the Wrath of God the Father because of the shed blood of God the Son. Christ Jesus has interceded for authentic Christians in order for them to avoid the Wrath of the Lord God Almighty. Authentic Christians should never be embarrassed that vengeance belongs to the God of the Holy Bible (Deuteronomy 32:35) because that is part of Who the Lord God Almighty is: It is part of His very nature and character.

Concerning end-time prophecies relative to the outpouring of God's Wrath, it is important for the spiritually-minded to understand that two major developments occur during the end-times. Both are already in the making. One is the formation of a ten-nationed United States of Europe (a ten-nation confederacy of European states). And the other is the formation of a ten-nationed Islamic Republic (a ten-nation confederacy of Islamic states).

The development of each confederacy (or "beast") is described in the last book of the Bible, the *Book of Revelation:*

The formation of a ten-nationed European Community — what many have come to call "the revived Holy Roman Empire" — is prophesied in the Seventeenth Chapter of the *Book of Revelation*. The formation of the ten-nationed Islamic Republic — what most people have failed to identify at all — is prophesied in Chapter Thirteen of the *Book of Revelation*. In those two chapters, two entirely different political, economic, and religious entities are each depicted as a beast having seven heads and ten horns. Although their similar depictions have prompted many Bible expositors to conclude that the beasts are one and the same, such a conclusion is incorrect. Though both have seven heads and ten horns, the "scarlet-colored beast" in Revelation 17 is not the same as the beast "like a leopard" in Revelation 13. That they each have seven heads and ten horns simply means they are both manifestations of evil — the Devil himself depicted in Revelation 12 as "a great red dragon, having seven heads and ten horns."

Following are Revelation 17 and 13 unlocked by the Holy Spirit to spiritual sense:

Revelation, Seventeenth Chapter

Verses 1 through 6

"And there came one of the seven angels who had the seven vials, and talked with me, saying unto me, 'Come here; I will show unto you the judgment of the great whore that sits upon many waters: With whom the kings of the earth have committed fornication, and the inhabitants of the earth have been made drunk with the wine of her fornication.' So he carried me away in the spirit into the wilderness: and I saw a woman sit upon a scarlet colored beast, full of names of blasphemy, having seven heads and ten horns. And the woman was arrayed in purple and scarlet color, and decked with gold and precious stones and pearls, having a golden cup in her hand full of abominations and filthiness of her fornication: And upon her forehead was a mysterious name written: BABYLON THE GREAT, THE MOTHER OF HARLOTS AND ABOMINATIONS [IDOLATRIES] OF THE EARTH."

"The great whore that sits upon many waters" is the Roman Catholic Church. That "the kings of the earth have committed fornication" with her refers to the joint rule she has enjoyed with many governments throughout the world over the past two millennia. That "the inhabitants of the earth have been made drunk with the wine of her fornication" means that, through her teachings, many tribes, nations, and people have been led to apostasy (that is, to worship for Christ what is not Christ and to follow error instead of truth). The scarlet and purple colors in which the woman is arrayed symbolize the whorish nature of her sovereign doctrine. That she is "decked with gold and precious stones and pearls" indicates her great material wealth. The "cup in her hand full of abominations and filthiness of her fornication" points to the golden chalice with which the Roman Catholic Church serves idolatry and false doctrine — *for example:* (1) in the "eucharist" of Christ's recurring sacrifice during its mass and (2) in its erroneous endorsement of Muslims as people who worship the God of the Holy Bible (see Statement 841 in Part One, Section Two, Third Chapter, Article Nine, Paragraph Three, and Roman Numeral Three of the *Catechism of the Catholic Church*). The name on her headband signifies her vice (which is to say, spiritual prostitution) and the extent to which that vice has spread. That she is "drunken with the blood of saints, and with the blood of the martyrs of Jesus" refers both to her delusion that, because many of her members are of God (i.e., authentic Christian believers), she also is of God. In other words, the Roman Catholic Church reels in the names of God's elect within her own organization to lend credibility to her corrupt and illegitimate institution.

Protestants beware! You should *not* discriminate against your Christian brothers and sisters who happen to be Roman Catholic. There have been, and still are, many fine authentic Christians in the Roman Catholic Church. Protestants who take delight in correctly pointing to the Roman Church as "the Whore of Babylon" should remember that, because she is also the "mother of harlots" (verse 6), there is sufficient manure to cover her "daughters," including Protestant denominations with their own gross doctrinal errors as well. There are not only Protestant denominations that are recognized as cults by mainstream Christianity but also Protestant denominations that are cults even though they are not recognized as such, including those who base salvation on *works* — such as falsely speaking in tongues, false prophesying, false signs, and false wonders. To be sure, speaking in tongues, prophesying, signs, and wonders still exist but not in or through immature Christians who pretend and invent their existence as a result of peer pressure, hypnotic influence, hysteria, self-delusion, and/or the desire to manipulate and exploit others.

Verses 7 through 8

"And the angel said to me, 'Why are you surprised? I will tell you the mystery of the woman, and of the beast that carries her, which has the seven heads and ten horns. The beast that you saw was, and is not; and shall ascend out of the bottomless pit, and go to destruction: and they that dwell on the earth shall wonder, whose names were not written in the book of life from the casting down of the world, when they behold the beast that was and is not, and yet is.'"

"The beast that you saw was, and is not" refers to the fallen Roman Empire. That the empire "shall ascend" means that it will rise again — "yet is" also indicating its presence looming on the horizon. "The bottomless pit" is the depths of corruption, Hades, or hell. That "those whose names were not written in the book of life" shall wonder means that unsaved souls will not understand the true significance of the Roman Empire's reemergence.

Verses 9 through 11

"'And here is the mind that has wisdom. The seven heads are seven mountains on which the woman sits. And there are seven kings: five are fallen, and one is, and the other is not yet come; and when he arrives, he must continue a short space. And the beast that was, and is not, even he is the eighth, and is of the seven, and goes to destruction.'"

"Seven heads" here carries a double meaning. First, it refers to the seven hills of Rome that are named *Aventine, Caelian, Capitoline, Esquiline, Palatine, Quirinal,* and *Viminal,* which surround the city of blasphemy "on which the woman sits;" and, second, it refers to the seven political systems ("seven kings") by which Rome has governed and been governed. That "five are fallen, and one is, and the other is not yet come" and the beast is "the eighth" and "of the seven" all point to the political systems being successive (one after the other) rather than all existing at the same time. *For example:*

1. The Republic of Rome
   510 B.C. - 476 A.D.
   (The last Roman emperor was deposed in 476 AD.)

2. The barbarian (foreign) rule of Rome
   476 A.D. - 774 A.D.

3. The Carolingian Empire and its legacy to Rome: The growth of Rome into a city-state and the development of joint rule by nobility and papacy
   774 A.D. - 1420 A.D.

4. Rome under absolute papal rule
   1420 A.D. - 1870 A.D.

5. Rome included within an Italian constitutional monarchy
   1870 A.D. - 1922 A.D.
   (This inclusion was heralded by the withdrawal of the French garrison supporting Pope Pius IX, the surrender of Rome to Italian troops, and the subsequent election of Rome as seat of the government.)

6. Rome under Italian Fascism
   1922 A.D. - 1946 A.D.

7. Rome as the seat of an Italian "democratic Republic"
   1946 A.D. - present
   (1948 was the actual year that the new constitution came into full force.)

8. Rome as the seat of the European Economic Community (EEC): Symbolized by the Treaty of Rome, signed on March 25, 1957 and put into force on January 1, 1958

Verses 12 through 18

"'And the ten horns that you saw are ten kings, which have received no kingdom as yet, but receive power as kings one hour with the beast. These have one mind, and shall give their power to the beast. These shall make war with the Lamb, and the Lamb shall overcome them: for he is Lord of Lords, and King of Kings: and they that are with him are called, and chosen, and faithful.' And he said to me: 'The waters which you saw, where the whore sits, are people, and multitudes, and nations, and tongues. And the ten horns that you saw upon the beast, these shall hate the whore, and shall make her desolate and naked, and shall eat her flesh, and burn her with fire. For God has put into their hearts to fulfill His Will, and to agree, and give their kingdoms unto the beast, until the words of God shall be fulfilled. And the woman that you saw is that great city, which reigns over the kings of the earth.'"

Here, it is clarified that ten nations ("ten kings") will arise as a union. That "these have one mind, and shall give their power and strength to the beast" indicates their strong commitment to the union. That these kings will reign from the union's establishment until the Messiah's return is revealed by the angel telling John that they "shall make war with the Lamb." That they "shall hate the whore" means there will be no room for any of the doctrines of Roman Catholicism (true as well as false) within the political ideology that unites these nations. Thus, it is because of their incompatibility with the whore that the nations "shall make her desolate and naked, and shall eat her flesh, and burn her with fire" — meaning, they will remove her power and wealth by plundering and destroying her. Afterwards, Vatican City — "that great city, which reigns over the kings of the earth" — shall be no more.

For those readers who are students of the Holy Bible and remember the verse that tells the people to come out of *Babylon* (i.e., leave the Roman Catholic Church), it is God who calls His people out of that church, not you or I. Christians are not to judge, condemn, or insult their Roman Catholic brothers and sisters:

> And I heard another voice from heaven, saying: "Come out of her, My people, that you are not partakers of her sins, and that you do not receive her plagues."
>
> *Revelation 18:4 KJV (Paraphrase)*

Revelation, Thirteenth Chapter

Verses 1 through 2

"And I saw a beast rise up out of the sea, having seven heads and ten horns, and upon his horns ten crowns, and upon his heads the name of blasphemy. And the beast which I saw was like a leopard, and his feet were as the feet of a bear, and his mouth as the mouth of a lion: and the dragon gave him his power, and his seat, and great authority."

This beast — the same beast that Daniel saw as the last of "four great beasts" (Daniel 7:3 KJV) — represents the most terrible empire the world will ever know. That the beast is "like a leopard" speaks of the cunning practices by which it will disrupt the entire Earth as well as the leopard's one-time indigenous association with (i.e., geographic dispersal in) both the Middle East and northern Africa. That the leopard's feet are "as the feet of a bear" means it will unmercifully trample and crush all who oppose it. That its mouth is "the mouth of a lion" identifies its devouring and scornful nature. Like the scarlet-colored beast of Revelation 17, the backbone of this beast will be a league of ten nations ("ten horns"). However, unlike the scarlet-colored beast of the Seventeenth Chapter of Revelation, full authority will be given to the leopard-like beast of the Thirteenth Chapter of Revelation during "the end-times." In short, the dragon's (or Devil's) final movements will be made through this beast: the so-called nation of Islam, a confederacy of Islamic states. It should be noted that —

because of the Roman Catholic Church's and Western Europe's support for Islam, Muslims, and the Koran (al-Qur'an) — the scarlet-colored beast of the Seventeenth Chapter of Revelation and the leopard-like beast of the Thirteenth Chapter of Revelation are intertwined. However, each of those two beasts is made up of a different set of ten nation-states.

Following is the present author's artistic rendering, drawn in 1979, of the Islamic beast from Revelation 13. ("Artistic rendering" here means that the drawing is a conceptual representation and, therefore, not meant to imply that this is what the Apostle John actually saw in his vision.)

Author's Artistic Rendering of the Beast

Figure Two

Eventually, some of the Islamic nations pictured on the following map in Figure Three will be part of the Islamic Confederacy referred to as *the leopard-like beast* in the Thirteenth Chapter of the Book of Revelation. (Islamic island nations in the Pacific South West are not shown in Figure Three.)

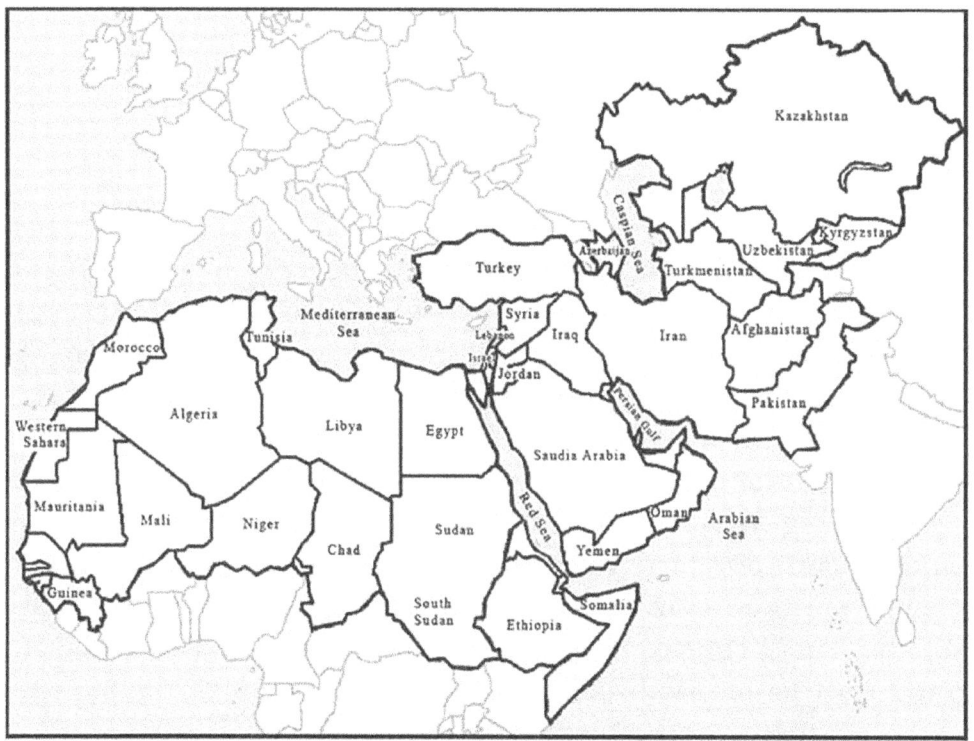

Prospective Nations Forming the Beast

Figure Three

In all likelihood, this Islamic Confederacy will include nations of the Middle East and Northern Africa, *for example:* Iran, Iraq, Turkey, Syria, Lebanon, Jordan, Saudi Arabia, Yemen, Egypt, and Libya. It is also likely that many of the nation-states in the Islamic Confederacy will include members of **OPEC** because of their economic bond. In 2020, countries on the map in Figure Three that are members of

OPEC include: Algeria, Iran, Iraq, Kuwait, Libya, Nigeria, Qatar, Arabia, and the United Arab Emirates. Although their borders are outlined on the map in Figure Three, Kuwait, Qatar, and the United Arab Emirates are too small to be labeled on this map. Kuwait is immediately southeast of Iraq. The U.A.E. is immediately north of Oman and east of Saudi Arabia. And Qatar is the small protrusion in the Persian Gulf immediately north of the U.A.E. and east of Saudi Arabia.

Verses 3 through 8

"And I saw one of his [the leopard-like beast's] heads as if it were wounded to death; and his deadly wound was healed: And all the world wondered about the [leopard-like] beast, and they worshiped the dragon because he gave power to the [leopard-like] beast. And they worshiped the [leopard-like] beast, saying, 'Who is like the beast? Who is able to make war with him?' And there was given unto him a mouth speaking great things and blasphemies; and power was given unto him to continue forty two months (three and one-half years). And he opened his mouth in blasphemy against God, to blaspheme His Name, and His Tabernacle, the ones dwelling in heaven. And it was given to him [the leopard-like beast] to make war with the saints, and to overcome them: and power was given him over all people, and languages, and nations. And all that dwell on the earth shall worship him, whose names are not written in the slain Lamb's book of life from the casting down of the world."

As the present author sees it, there are three possible explanations for the healing of the deadly wound of the leopard-like beast:

(1) The first possibility is that the wounding and healing of one of the leopard-like beast's heads may refer to the miraculous deathbed recovery that one of the new empire's rulers will make (the phrase "by a sword" — used to qualify "wound" in verse Revelation 13:14 — suggests that the leader will be "pierced" in an assassination attempt).

(2) The second possibility is that the wounding and healing of one of the leopard-like beast's heads may refer to the reunification of the Sunnah and Shia sects of Islam through the healing of the doctrinal schism between them.

(3) The third possibility is that the wounding and healing of one of the leopard-like beast's heads may refer to the reunification of two or more countries that had once been joined to one another geographically, politically, and culturally: *for example,* the eventual rejoining of Iraq, Syria, Lebanon, and other adjacent countries prompted by the actions of the terrorist organization known by these three synonymous names: the *Islamic State* (IS), the *Islamic State of Iraq and Syria/al-Sham* (ISIS), and the *Islamic State of Iraq and the Levant* (ISIL). Interestingly, depending on which nations adjacent to the Mediterranean are included as "the Levant," IS/ISIS/ISIL may be the catalyst for joining or re-joining the ten nation-states that will then constitute the leopard-like beast of Revelation's Thirteenth Chapter. Many of the Middle East countries depicted in Figure Three were dissected from the Ottoman Empire by Great Britain and France (with endorsement from Russia) during World War I. Consequently, most militant Muslims and Jihadis view their current national borders as artificial and illegitimate. The extent of the Ottoman Empire in 1683 is shown in Figure Four. Although the western portion of Iran (separated by the dark jagged line in Figure Four on page 78) was not part of the Ottoman Empire, it is included here because: (1) this area was part of the Rashidun Caliphate in the late 7th century; and (2) strong cultural connections have existed between the Medo-Persians and the Assyrians and Syrians throughout much of recorded history.

Attempting to resurrect and expand the glory of the early Islamic caliphates as well as the Ottoman Empire, the ambitions of the Islamic State (IS/ISIS/ISIL) are shown in an unofficial map of the desired extent of its Caliphate in Figure Five on page 79. Undoubtedly, a final map of the Islamic beast described in the Thirteenth Chapter of the Book of Revelation will be drawn using many of the areas depicted in Figure Five irrespective of the exact names and exact borders of the included ten nation-states.

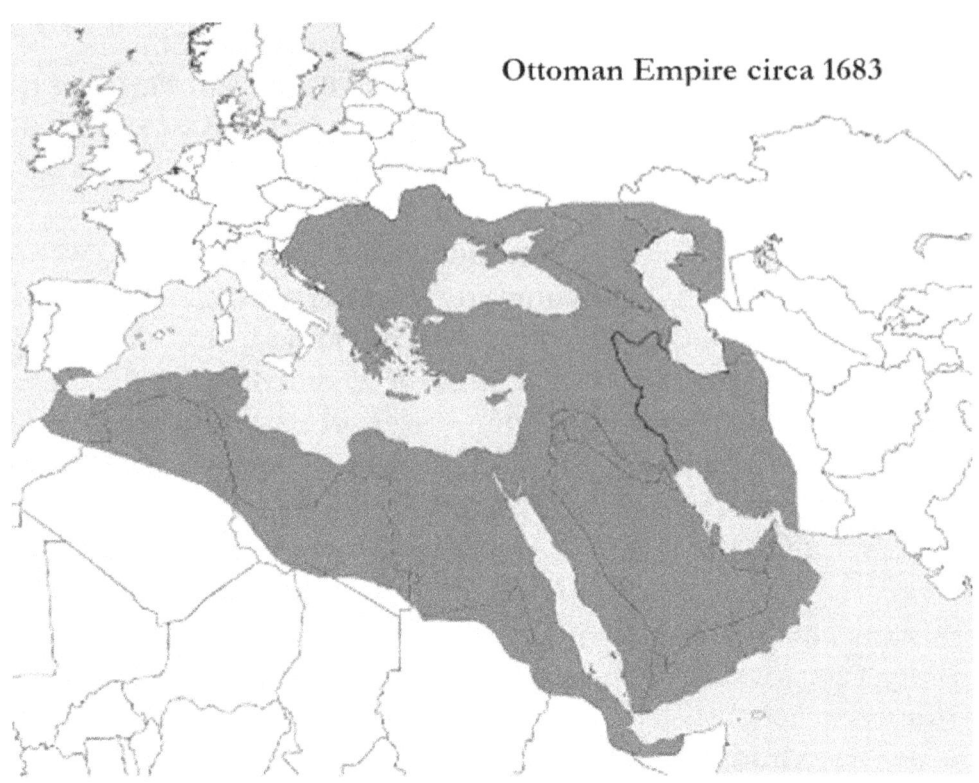

Ottoman Empire circa 1683

Figure Four

That "all the world wondered after the beast" signifies that the entire Earth will hold the terrorist confederacy of Islam in awe because of its consummate power. That "they worshiped the beast" simply means that all nations will eventually bow before the power it wields and, thus, prostrate themselves before the dragon (i.e., the Devil). In other words, by worshiping the earthly manifestation of evil, mortals will be worshiping Satan, who is the source of all evil. Therefore, although all people whose names are "not written in the book of life" will wonder at both the "scarlet-colored beast" (the European confederacy) and the "leopard-like beast" (the confederacy centered in the Middle East), worldwide amazement will turn to admiration and adoration during the latter times primarily in the case of the leopard-like Islamic beast (compare Revelation 13:8 with Revelation 17:8).

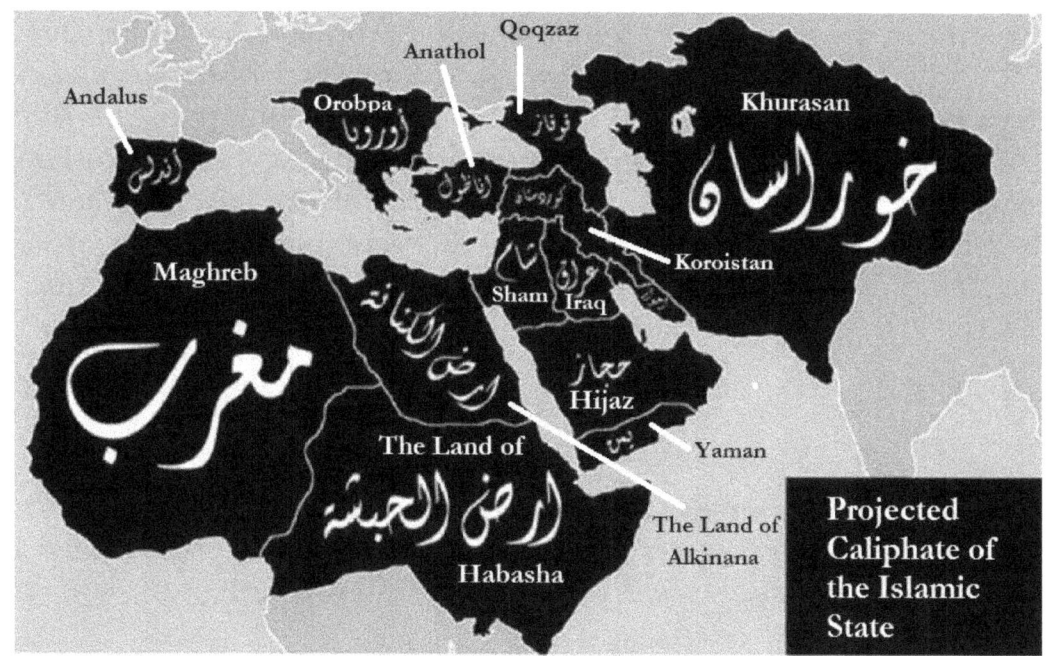

Projected Caliphate of the Islamic State

Figure Five

That the leopard-like Islamic beast will "make war with the saints" refers to the great wave of persecution that will follow those on this Earth who belong to the one true and only real God. That he will "wear out" (Daniel 7:25 KJV) and "overcome" the saints means that many Jews and Christians will be persecuted, terrorized, assaulted, turned out, starved, imprisoned, and murdered (especially through beheading) by those who have the mark of the beast or his name (i.e., those who worship *Allah* or work on behalf of Islam and Islam's founding false prophet, Mohammed).

That power was given to the leopard-like Islamic beast "to continue forty and two months" refers to the time remaining for this last earthly empire from the moment that it establishes "the abomination of desolation spoken of by Daniel" (Matthew 24:15; Mark 13:14) — "the abomination of desolation" translated from the Hebrew as "the transgression of desolation" and "the abomination that makes desolate" in the King James Version of that prophet's book (see Daniel 8:13, 11:31, and 12:11). The Hebrew word translated as "abomination" refers to something *detestable,* which, in the vocabulary of the Bible, is the worship of a false god through idolatrous practices. These idolatrous practices — including the sacrifice of animals, Jews, and/or Christians to Allah — have the potential to be conducted on or near Rock Moriah under the Dome of the Rock (the so-called Mosque of Omar).

Verses 9 through 10

"If anyone has an ear, let that person hear. He who leads into captivity shall go into captivity: he who kills with the sword must be killed with the sword. Here is the patience and the faith of the saints."

Here, John makes a direct reference to the spiritual law regarding Judgment that was expressed by the Holy Spirit to the Prophet Jeremiah: "Such as are for the famine, to the famine; and such as are for the captivity, to the captivity" (Jeremiah 15:2 KJV) — which spiritual law is also referred to by Christ Jesus: "All they that take the sword shall perish with the sword" (Matthew 26:52 KJV). In other words, those who have spiritual understanding are told that they will find the strength necessary to endure all pain and suffering if they remind themselves of that spiritual law.

Although the righteous on this Earth may be tempted to pay back men and women of violence with violence, they stand forewarned that such violence is against God and will be judged accordingly. Mortals are not to determine punishment. Vengeance belongs only to the God of the Holy Bible. Hence, although the sword may precede the word of Islam, children of God are to keep their peace during the forthcoming global jihad and know that, at the appointed time, justice shall proceed from the mouth of God by His sword alone. God's Justice and Judgment shall prevail! (This does not mean that people should refrain from defending themselves.)

Verses 11 through 15

"And I saw another beast [a second beast] coming up out of the earth; and he had two horns like a lamb, but he spoke as a dragon. And he exercised all the power of the first beast [the leopard-like beast] before him, and caused the earth and those who dwell therein to worship the first beast, whose 'deadly wound was healed' (Revelation 13:3). And he performed miracles, so that he made fire come down from heaven on the earth in the sight of men, and deceived them that dwell on the earth, that they should make an image to the [leopard-like, or first] beast, which had the wound by a sword, and did live. And he had power to give life unto the image of the [leopard-like, or first] beast, that the image of the [leopard-like, or first] beast should both speak, and to cause as many as would not worship the image of the [leopard-like, or first] beast to be killed."

That the second beast of Revelation 13 "had two horns like a lamb, but he spoke as a dragon" and that "he made fire come down from heaven" (as the Prophet Elijah did) identifies him as the great impostor, — the master of deception, — the grand imitator, — the man of whom "all men shall speak well" (Luke 6:26 KJV), — Islam's final false prophet, — the end-time Antichrist, — and Islam's long-awaited *Mahdi*. That he will exercise "all the power of the first beast" and cause "the earth and those who dwell therein to worship the first beast" further identifies him as the leading proponent of Islam during the latter days. Through this charismatic and scornful character, the inhabitants of this world will be deceived to pay homage to the Devil instead of to the Lord God Almighty.

The present author believes that *the image* of the leopard-like, or first, beast (i.e., *the idol of desolation*) will be a massive high definition video or holographic image of the Antichrist on the Jerusalem Temple Mount that regularly broadcasts blasphemies against the one true and only real God by: (1) offering praise to (a) the false god *Allah* (such as "Bismillah" and "Allahu Akbar"), (b) the leopard-like beast of Islam, and (c) Islam's founding false prophet,

Mohammed; as well as (2) making pronouncements and declarations that are against Jesus Christ. To be sure, all whose names are not written in the Lamb's *Book of Life* will worship the false god *Allah*. (For the sake of clarity, the *Lamb of God* is Christ Jesus and the *Book of Life* contains the names of those who have been saved by his blood.)

Verses 16 through 18

"And he caused all, both small and great, rich and poor, free and bond, to receive a mark in their right hand, or in their foreheads: And that no man might buy or sell, unless he had the mark or the name of the [leopard-like, or first] beast or the number of his name. Here is wisdom. Let the person who has understanding count the number of the [leopard-like, or first] beast: for it is the number of a man; and his number is six hundred threescore and six."

Here, it is indicated that only those who worship the god of Islam (i.e., have "the mark in their foreheads") and those who work on behalf of Islam (i.e., have "the mark in their right hands") during the latter times — or who have *Mohammed* ("the name of the beast") as one of their own names (*either de facto or de jure*) — will be able to carry out the simplest transactions necessary for daily living. (See Table One in Chapter Four of this book for proof that the number of the Islamic beast is signified by the name *Mohammed*.)

During the Tribulation (the seven year period that immediately precedes Jesus Christ's return to Earth), expect an increase in the systematic murdering of those who belong to the God of the Holy Bible (i.e., Jews and Christians), particularly through beheading:

"And I saw thrones, and they sat upon them, and judgment was given unto them: and I saw the souls of those who were beheaded for the witness of Jesus, and for the word of God, and which had not worshiped the beast, neither his image, neither had received his mark upon their foreheads, or in their hands;

and they lived and reigned with Christ a thousand years."
Revelation 20:4 KJV

Although all saints of the Lord God Almighty are equally justified (i.e., made the same in righteousness by the shed blood of Jesus Christ), all Christian martyrs are truly "first estate" Christians because of their unique sacrifice. Not denying Jesus Christ to avoid execution is undeniable evidence of remarkable trust in the God of the Holy Bible! To be sure, these Christian witnesses through martyrdom deserve to reign with Jesus Christ during the Millennium that begins with his bodily return to Earth. And, not only do they deserve to reign with him, they *will* reign with him as co-heirs.

Raising a Banner for Christian Truth

Religious Jews lay claim to the Biblical truth contained within Deuteronomy 6:4 and known as the *Shema:* "Hear, [O] Israel, *the Lord* (Yahweh) is our God, *the Lord* (Yahweh) is One," or "Hear, [O] Israel, *the Lord* (Yahweh) is our God, *the Lord* (Yahweh) alone." (As mentioned in the Fourth Chapter of this book, to avoid speaking the holy name *Yahweh* aloud, Jews are more likely to use one of the following appellations instead: *Adonai, Lord, HaShem,* or *the Name.*)

Muslims profess their fundamental beliefs in a parody statement known as the *Shahada* (or "testimony") — also known as the *Shahadatan* (i.e., "two testimonials," referring to the two independent clauses in the following compound sentence): "There is no god but Allah, and Mohammed is the messenger of Allah." When spoken, this statement is often used by Muslims as evidence of a professing faith in the pagan god Allah and/or evidence of an unbeliever's conversion to

Islam. (For those of you who are willing to vocalize the Muslim *Shahada* in order to avoid execution, history demonstrates that you may still be beheaded as an infidel by Jihadis even after repeating it.)

The banners in Figures Six and Seven demonstrate the present author's Christian embrace of the Jewish *Shema* as well as repudiation of the Muslim *Shahada*. My Christian testimony states in Arabic: "There is no Creator but Jehovah (Yahweh), and Jesus Christ is His *only-begotten* Son" (Figure Six), and in Hebrew: "There is no Creator-God but Yahweh, and Y'shua H'Moshiach is His *only-begotten* Son" (Figure Seven). (Concerning the Hebrew spelling of Y'shua in Figure Seven, I have used the spelling that is more common in secular contexts because I especially want this banner's message to speak to those Jews who are not yet saved: The Hebrew spelling of *Y'shua* that I have used unquestionably conveys to modern Israelis "Jesus of Nazareth" and no other Jesus.)

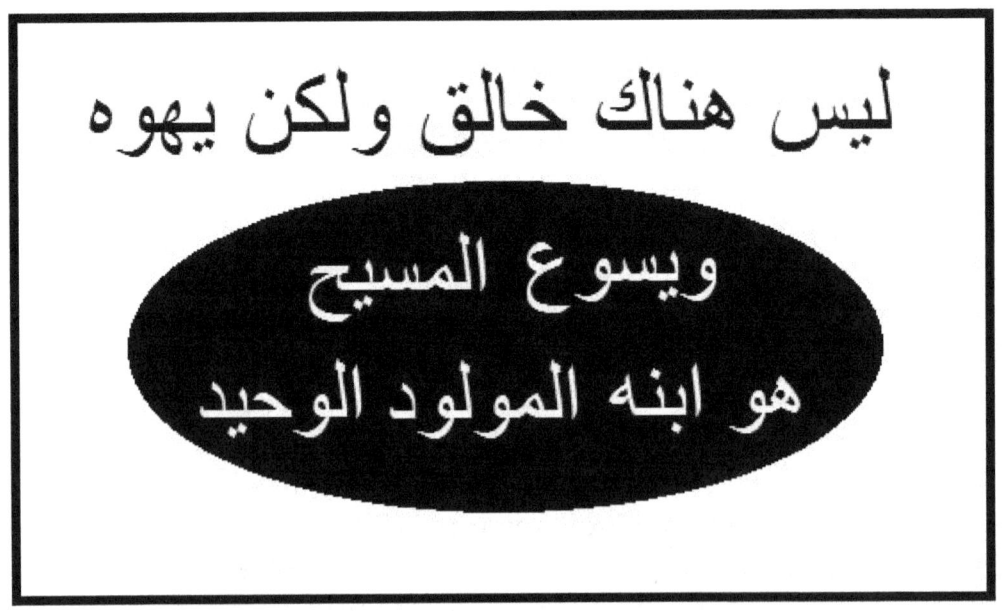

Figure Six

Figure Seven

Let us pray that each authentic Christian always finds the unwavering courage to proclaim the fundamental truth expressed by these banners.

CHAPTER SIX
The Worst Woes

Introduction

In 1979, I heard an audible voice from Heaven that said: "The worst woes will come to those who heap their grief by blood of sheep." I knew immediately that this was a prophetic message sent to me from the God of the Holy Bible via a heavenly messenger. In retrospect, I now know that the message was given to me so I might research its meaning in the Holy Bible and gradually come to understand what is now embodied in this work, entitled "Revelation of Antichrist." [The earliest editions of this work were copyrighted as "The Koran (al-Qur'an): Testimony of Antichrist."]

It has taken me many years to complete my work based on this message. In fact, I still receive spiritual insights clarifying various aspects of end-time events related to this message. As I see it, this information, and information like it, will one day be illegal to possess and openly share because it is critical of Islam. I believe that all major governments will eventually give in to pressure from international human rights groups, Islamic governments, and even the United Nations to criminalize spoken and written criticism of all religions for the seemingly benevolent purpose of global unity through political, national, and ethnic peace and harmony. Such criminalization of the free press will only help Islam and hurt Christianity. Satan has worked tirelessly toward this end because Islam cannot stand up to the scrutiny of those who know and understand real Scripture. (Again, for the sake of clarity, the Holy Bible is the only real Scripture.)

Please be informed that anyone who claims as their own my "worst woes" quote or my cryptographic Hebrew spelling of Mohammed and its numerical equivalents adding up to 666 (given in the five steps of Table One of this book and explained further in Appendix A) has plagiarized them. To prove my ownership of these most important elements, I have kept my earliest manuscript submissions to the United States Copyright Office and their certificates of copyright awarded in 1981 and 1989.

An 1989 edition of this book still exists on the internet (in 2020) at: www.archive.org/details/TheKoranTestamonyOfTheAntichrist. (Please note that the misspelling of "Testimony" on this URL is the work of the person who, without my solicitation, uploaded my earlier work to www. archive.org.) In the final analysis, I do not mind that an earlier copyrighted version has been thus archived because it helps to attest to the history of this evolving work's existence in the public eye.

After I heard the heavenly voice, I recognized that the "worst woes" statement refers to God's Wrath brought about by the last three angelic trumpets — trumpet five, trumpet six, and trumpet seven — referred to in Revelation 8:13 (KJV) as "Woe, woe, woe" (Greek "Οὐαὶ οὐαὶ οὐαὶ"). The Greek οὐαὶ (pronounced ü-ī') [G3759] has its origin in the Hebrew word *'owy* [H188] (see Table Two in Chapter Four), which is found, *for example,* in Numbers 21:29, 1 Samuel 4:7, and Isaiah 3:11, and from which the Yiddish "oy" is also derived:

> And I saw, and heard an angel flying through the midst of heaven, saying with a loud voice, "Woe, woe, woe to the inhabitants of the earth by reason of the other voices of the trumpet of the three angels, which are yet to sound!"
> *Revelation 8:13 KJV*

The first two woes sounded by the fifth and sixth angelic trumpets will certainly include latter-day Muslims, but the third woe and its associated seven plagues, sounded by the seventh angelic trumpet, will fall almost exclusively on latter-day Muslims. All three woes referred to in Revelation 8:13 are detailed in the Ninth and Sixteenth Chapters of the Book of Revelation.

The three woes from Revelation 8:13 are summarized as follows:

The Fifth Trumpet

Revelation 9: Verses 1 through 12

"{1} And the fifth angel sounded, and I saw a star fall from heaven to the earth: and to him was given the key of the bottomless pit. {2} And he opened the bottomless pit; and there arose a smoke out of the pit, as the smoke of a great furnace; and the sun and the air were darkened by reason of the smoke of the pit. {3} And there came out of the smoke locusts upon the earth: and unto them was given power, as the scorpions of the earth have power. {4} And it was commanded them that they should not hurt the grass of the earth, neither any green thing, neither any tree; but only those people who do not have the seal of God in their foreheads. {5} And to them it was given that they should not kill them, but that they should be tormented five months: and their torment was as the torment of a scorpion, when he strikes a man. {6} And in those days shall people seek death, and shall not find it; and shall desire to die, and death shall flee from them. {7} And the shapes of the locusts were like horses prepared unto battle; and on their heads were as it were crowns like gold, and their faces were as the faces of men. {8} And they had hair as the hair of women, and their teeth were as the teeth of lions. {9} And they had breastplates, as it were breastplates of iron; and the sound of their wings was as the sound of chariots of many horses running to battle. {10} And they had tails like unto scorpions, and there were stings in their tails: and their power was to hurt people five months. {11} And they had a king over them, which is the angel of the bottomless pit, whose name in the Hebrew tongue is Abaddon, but in the Greek tongue is his name Apollyon [the god of war and terror]. {12} One woe is past; and, behold, there come two woes more hereafter."

The first "woe" referred to in Revelation 8:13 will plague the earth and torment "only those people who do not have the seal of God in their foreheads" [i.e., God's Holy Spirit] (Revelation 9:4 KJV). Such pestilence will occur for a period of "five months" (Revelation 9:5 KJV and 9:10 KJV), most likely during the second three-and-one-half years of the seven-year Tribulation. This second period of three-and-one-half years is often referred to as the "Great Tribulation" (from Revelation 7:14 KJV).

> ... in those days shall people seek death, and shall not find it; and shall desire to die, and death shall flee from them.
> *Revelation 9:6 KJV*

Thus, the tormenting woe described in Revelation 9:1-12 is conceptually similar to the hemorrhoids with which the Lord God Almighty struck the Philistines:

> And the men that died not were smitten with the emerods [hemorrhoids]: and the cry of the city went up to heaven.
> *1 Samuel 5:12 KJV*

The first of the three woes is "conceptually similar" to the hemorrhoids of 1 Samuel 5:12 because that woe will torment but not kill. The agents of the woe heralded by the trumpet of the fifth angel are described in Revelation 9:3, 5, and 7-10 as horse-like locusts with stings like scorpions. Because this Biblical description is figurative, the exact agents will remain unclear until the time when this particular plague of locusts is dispensed.

The Sixth Trumpet

Revelation 9: Verses 13 through 21

"{13} And the sixth angel sounded, and I heard a voice from the four horns of the golden altar which is before God, {14} saying to the sixth angel which had the trumpet, 'Loose the four angels which are bound in the great river Euphrates.' [Author's Note: The Euphrates River runs through modern-day Turkey, Syria, and Iraq.] {15} And the four angels were loosed, which were prepared for an hour, and a day, and a month, and a year, in order to slay the third part of people. {16} And the number of the army of the horsemen were two hundred thousand thousand: and I heard the number of them. {17} And thus I saw the horses in the vision, and them that sat on them, having breastplates of fire, and of jacinth, and brimstone: and the heads of the horses were as the heads of lions; and out of their mouths issued fire and smoke and brimstone. {18} By these three was the third part of people killed, by the fire, and by the smoke, and by the brimstone, which issued out of their mouths. {19} For their power is in their mouth, and in their tails: for their tails were like unto serpents, and had heads, and with them they do harm. {20} And the rest of the men which were not killed by these plagues yet repented not of the works of their hands, that they should not worship devils, and idols of gold, and silver, and brass, and stone, and of wood: which neither can see, nor hear, nor walk: {21} Neither repented they of their murders, nor of their sorceries, nor of their fornication, nor of their thefts."

As indicated, the second "woe" referred to in Revelation 8:13 will kill one-third of all humankind:

> By these three was the third part of all people killed: by the fire, and by the smoke, and by the brimstone...
>
> *Revelation 9:18 KJV*

Perhaps the three elements of "fire," "smoke," and "brimstone" represent effects from nuclear, chemical, and/or biological warfare. Or perhaps these three elements represent excessive heat from explosive devices and their related harmful burning odors and toxic vapors. To be sure, although the description of the three elements of this woe is less figurative than the description of their agents — which are described in Revelation 9:17 & 19 as lion-headed horses with serpent-headed tails — the exact elements as well as their agents will remain unclear until the time when this particular plague is dispensed. The likelihood of warfare as the means for this second woe is great because of the description of warrior-like "horsemen" with "breastplates" in Revelation 9:17. Like the first woe, time will clarify the exact nature of the plagues for this second woe.

The Seventh Trumpet
(Revelation 10:7; 11:14-19; 15:1; 16:1-21)

The third and final "woe" referred to in Revelation 8:13 is released from the seven vials, bowls, or flasks of plagues, primarily described in Revelation 16:1-21.

Revelation 16: Verses 1 through 21

"{1} And I heard a great voice out of the temple saying to the seven angels, 'Go your ways, and pour out the vials of the Wrath of God upon the earth.' {2} And the first went, and poured out his vial upon the earth; and there fell a noisome and grievous sore upon the people who had the mark of the beast, and upon those who worshiped his image. {3} And the second angel poured out his vial upon the sea; and it became as the blood of a dead man: and every living soul died in the sea. {4} And the third angel poured out his vial upon the rivers and fountains of waters; and they became blood. {5} And I heard the angel of the waters say, 'You are righteous, O Lord, [You] who are, and was, and ever shall be, because You have judged in this way. {6} For they have shed the blood of saints and prophets, and You have given them blood to drink; for they are worthy.' {7} And I heard another out of the altar say, 'Even so, Lord God Almighty, true and righteous are Your judgments.' {8} And the fourth angel poured out his vial upon the sun; and power was given unto the sun to scorch people with fire. {9} And people were scorched with great heat, and blasphemed the name of God, which has power over these plagues: and they repented not and did not give Him glory. {10} And the fifth angel poured out his vial upon the seat of the beast; and his kingdom was full of darkness; and they gnawed their tongues for pain, {11} And blasphemed the God of heaven because of their pains and their sores, and repented not of their deeds. {12} And the sixth angel poured out his vial upon the great river Euphrates; and it was dried up, that the way of the kings of the east might be prepared. {13} And I saw three unclean spirits like frogs come out of the mouth of the dragon, and out of the mouth of the beast, and out of the mouth of the false prophet. {14} For they are the spirits of devils, working miracles, which go forth unto the kings of the earth and of the whole world, to gather them to the battle of that great day of God Almighty. {15} Behold, I [the Lord Jesus Christ] come as a thief. Blessed is the person who watches, and keeps his garments, so that he does not walk naked, and they see his shame. {16} And he gathered them together into a place called in the Hebrew tongue Armageddon. {17} And the seventh angel poured out his vial into the air; and there came a great voice out of the temple of heaven, from the throne, saying, 'It is done.' {18} And there were voices, and thunders, and lightnings; and there was a great earthquake, such as was not since people were first upon the earth, so mighty an earthquake, and so great. {19} And the great city [Jerusalem] was divided into three parts, and the cities of the nations fell: and great Babylon [Vatican City in Rome] came in remembrance before God, to give to her the cup of the wine of the fierceness of His wrath. {20} And every island fled away, and the mountains were not found. {21} And there fell upon men a great hail out of heaven, every stone about the weight of a talent [a *talent* is equal to 60 kilograms or 130 pounds]: and men blasphemed

God because of the plague of the hail; for the plague thereof was exceedingly great."

The primary impact of the plagues in Revelation 16 is on latter-day Muslims. In effect, those who terrorize and destroy the Earth (or aid and abet those who terrorize and destroy the Earth) will themselves be terrorized and destroyed (Revelation 11:18). Revelation 16:6 pinpoints that those who distance themselves the furthest from God are those who "have shed the blood of saints and prophets." Hence, "the worst woes will come to those who heap their grief (i.e., widen their separation from the one true and only real God) by [spilling the] blood of sheep." (*Sheep* here refers to "the people of God" and includes both Jews and Christians.)

In Revelation 16, people who receive the Wrath of God in these last seven plagues are characterized as those who: (1) refuse to acknowledge the God of the Holy Bible as the one true and only real God; and (2) refuse to repent of their blasphemies against Him. The same characterizations are found in Revelation 9:20-21. (Remember, *steadfastly maintaining* that God does not have an *only-begotten* Son is the ultimate blasphemy against the God of the Holy Bible.) For their hardened hearts and ungodly actions, these unrepentant sinners confirm that God's Wrath upon them is just and justified. Indeed, the Wrath of God shall rain down upon those not sealed by God's Holy Spirit — which is to say, upon those who have rejected the Lord God Almighty by rejecting His *only-begotten* Son! The fire of God's Wrath shall burn until there is no more fuel for it. In other words, blasphemies against God fuel His Fiery Wrath until the blasphemies are expunged and, therefore, cease to exist.

Paradoxically, the plague upon the sun by the fourth angel, described in Revelation 16:8-9, causes the sun to scorch people with fire and heat. In all probability, the fire and heat will come from the unprecedented strength and increased number of future coronal mass ejections (CMEs) from our Sun. Coronal mass ejections come from the collisions of magnetic field lines on the Sun and have significant correlation with strong solar flares and multiple sunspots. The dangerous energy from coronal mass ejections reaches Earth within three to five days after their initial eruption. Because they impact the Earth's magnetosphere and ionosphere, coronal mass ejections: (1) can permanently impair transformers associated with power grids worldwide; (2) can cause changes in weather patterns due to alternating blasts from arctic air and equatorial air that result in seriously damaging megastorms (i.e., hurricanes, cyclones, and tornadoes); and (3) can cause sudden tectonic plate shifts that result in earthquakes, volcanoes, tsunamis, and significant coastal and inland flooding. To gain greater insights, please read and review what has already been written and videotaped concerning "coronal mass ejections" on the internet.

Although learning about coronal mass ejections won't be able to change the future, learning about them will help you to understand some of the future changes prophesied in Scripture. Therefore, you will be better equipped mentally, emotionally, spiritually, and even physically. (God always wants His people to be better prepared for the future.) *For example,* the following prophecy about the Sun and Moon is linked to coronal mass ejections:

> Moreover the light of the Moon [i.e., reflected light and energy] shall be as the light of the Sun, and the light of the Sun shall be sevenfold, as the light of seven days, in the day that the Lord binds up the breach of His people, and heals the stroke of their wound.
>
> *Isaiah 30:26 KJV*

The Sixteenth Chapter concludes with a plague of heavy hailstones: These hailstones are meteorites that fall on lands where people continue to reject Christ Jesus as Savior of the world, personal Savior, and God's *only-begotten* Son.

God's Judgment on the Beast of Islam
Revelation 19:19-21

Finally, what becomes of the nation of Islam, its confederacy of nation-states, and unrepentant Muslims is summarized in Revelation 19:19-21:

"{19} And I saw the beast, and the kings of the earth, and their armies, gathered together to make war against him that sat on the horse, and against his army. [He who "sat on the horse" is identified in Revelation 19:13 as "the Word of God" and in 19:16 as "King of kings and Lord of lords." Both are titles for Jesus Christ.] {20} And the beast was taken, and with him the false prophet that wrought miracles before him [in homage to the beast], with which he [the false prophet] deceived them that had received the mark of the beast [i.e., unrepentant Muslims as well as all who support Islam], and them that worshiped his image [i.e., the "abomination of desolation," or "idol of destruction," spoken of by the Prophet Daniel in Daniel 11:31 and 12:11 and by Jesus Christ in Matthew 24:15 and Mark 13:14]. These both [i.e., the beast and the false prophet] were cast alive into a Lake of Fire burning with brimstone. {21} And the remaining people [i.e., unrepentant Muslims and all who support Islam] were slain with the sword of him that sat upon the horse, which sword proceeded out of his mouth: and all the birds were filled with their flesh [by feeding on it]."

A Note of Clarification

Even though they are interdependent, the first beast in the Thirteenth Chapter of Revelation (i.e., the leopard-like beast introduced in Revelation 13:1 that arises out of the sea) is different from the second beast in the same chapter (i.e., the two-horned beast introduced in Revelation 13:11 that arises out of the earth). Because the first beast in the Thirteenth Chapter of Revelation has multiple meanings, the first beast is ambiguous to the casual reader or beginning student of the Book of Revelation. To the present author, the first "beast" in the Thirteenth Chapter has these, often simultaneous, multiple meanings: (1) the ideology of Islam; (2) the "nation," or caliphate, of Islam; (3) a confederacy of Islamic nation-states centered in the Middle East, Western Asia, and Northern Africa; and (4) the founding false prophet of Islam, Mohammed. Thus, the original promulgator of Islam, Mohammed, is just as synonymous with the "first beast" in the Thirteenth Chapter of Revelation as the ideology, politics, and geography of Islam are synonymous with the "first beast." In contrast, the "second beast" in the Thirteenth Chapter of Revelation is less ambiguous because the "second beast" represents the final false prophet of Islam — which is to say, the end-time Antichrist. Thus, as interpreted by the present author, the two living beings (i.e., entities with souls) — referred to in Revelation 19:20 KJV as "the beast" and "the false prophet" — that are thrown into the Lake of Fire are: (1) the founding false prophet of Islam, Mohammed; and (2) the final false prophet of Islam, the end-time Antichrist. These two are the only beings thrown into the Lake of Fire at the time of the return of Christ Jesus to rule on Earth. Any others destined for the Lake of Fire will be sent there at the end of the Millennial reign of Jesus Christ, approximately 1,000 years after the founding false prophet and the final false prophet have been sent there. As indicated in Revelation 19:21, all human followers of Satan, Islam, Mohammed, and the end-time Antichrist will be slain by the sword of Christ Jesus and removed from Earth at the time that he returns to establish his Millennial Kingdom.

In Summary

Although people may be polite, courteous, gracious, and hospitable, those traits and characteristics alone do not permit entrance to the

Kingdom of God. Such entree is provided only for repentant people who recognize and accept the shed blood of God's *only-begotten* Son as the sole means of atonement for their personal sins and for the remission (cancellation) of the personal debt they owe for their sins. Without such recognition and acceptance, God's Holy Spirit cannot indwell human beings, and, for that reason, such unbelieving people are easily deceived into worshiping a false god.

Because they worship Satan and openly reject Jesus Christ as God Incarnate as well as the *only-begotten* Son of God, Muslims carry a curse with them wherever they go. Peace cannot exist for Muslims or with Muslims because they all carry the same curse. A curse from the God of the Holy Bible remains upon them as long as they reject Jesus Christ as God Incarnate and the *only-begotten* Son of the God of the Holy Bible. (Remember, the Islamic *Allah* is NOT the God of the Holy Bible. The Islamic *Allah* is Satan in disguise.)

Muslims declare that nowhere in the Holy Bible does Jesus Christ state "I am God." However, Jesus said "I am Alpha and Omega, the Beginning and the End, the First and the Last" (Revelation 22:13). As stated previously, according to the unified language of the Holy Bible, saying "I am the First and Last" is equivalent to saying "I am God." *For example,* in Isaiah 41:4, the God of the Holy Bible states: "Who has wrought and done it, calling the generations from the beginning? I the LORD, the First, and the Last; I am He." And in Isaiah 44:6, the God of the Holy Bible states: "Thus says the LORD the King of Israel, and his [Israel's] redeemer the LORD of hosts; I am the First, and I am the Last; and beside Me there is no God." In their stubborn pride, Muslims refuse to recognize that God the Father, God the Son, and God the Holy Spirit are all coequal parts of the Godhead. Indeed, God the Father, God the Son, and God the Holy Spirit are *homoousion* — meaning, they constitute the three parts of the one Supreme Being consubstantially united. To be sure, God the Son delivers the entire Earth to God the Father at the end of his 1,000 year reign on Earth as described in 1 Corinthians 15:24-28 — supporting the understanding that the Godhead is currently partitioned in order to effect the Plan of Salvation that is articulated in the Holy Bible.

Finally, Muslims also declare that nowhere in the Holy Bible does Jesus Christ state "I am the Son of God." However, Scripture has recorded that "he [Jesus] trusted in God; let Him deliver him now, if He will have him: for he said, 'I am the Son of God'" (Matthew 27:43 KJV). And "do you say of him, whom the Father has sanctified, and sent into the world, 'You blaspheme' because I [Jesus] said, 'I am the Son of God?'" (John 10:36 KJV) Unfortunately, when faced with Bible-based refutations to their ideology, the response from Muslims eventually defaults to this refrain: "The Bible has been corrupted. Therefore, we cannot, and will not, believe what it says, especially when it contradicts the Koran (al-Qur'an)."

CHAPTER SEVEN

Clarifications concerning the Antichrist

It is evident to the present author that the end-time ruler referred to in the Book of Daniel, that soon-to-be-revealed "man of sin, — the son of perdition" (2 Thessalonians 2:3 KJV), will be a follower of Mohammed: "even him, whose coming is after the workings of Satan with all power and signs and lying wonders" (2 Thessalonians 2:9 KJV). The end-time Antichrist will be one with, and the same as, the second beast whom the Apostle John described as "having two horns like a lamb, yet speaking as a dragon" (Revelation 13:11 KJV). It is he who will be the one to "exercise all the power of the first beast before him, and cause the earth and them that dwell therein to worship the first beast" (Revelation 13:12 KJV), such first beast collectively being Islam, its confederacy of nation states, its ideology, and its founding false prophet, Mohammed.

Was the original Mohammed himself the end-time Antichrist? No. Mohammed produced the Koran (al-Qur'an), which is testimony of the Antichrist (that to which the end-time Antichrist will lay claim in order to authenticate himself as a spokesperson for Allah). Thus, Mohammed was the primogenitor of the end-time Antichrist (in that sense, the two are one). Yet to come, however, is a final false prophet (i.e., pseudo-religious, political leader) who will be the end-time Antichrist. He will stand in the founding false prophet's place.

How will we know when the end-time Antichrist has come? When mosques overflow in many lands and when, in cities and towns all over the Earth, laws are enacted that forbid buildings to be as high as, or higher than, the minaret of the mosque. To those who will be living at such a time, I repeat two things that have been told to me from Heaven: (1) "Beware of the man of whom all men speak well." (Read Luke 6:26 KJV.) And (2) "The worst woes will come to those who heap their grief by blood of sheep." (Read Revelation 8:13 through 11:15, 14:6 through 14:12, and 15:1 through 16:21 for a detailed account of those woes.) To be sure, understanding prophetic Scripture inculcates trust, protection, and assurance in the children of God because such understanding adds to "the patience and faith of the saints" (Revelation 13:10 KJV).

Time will show that Islam is Satan's religion of choice. Indeed, Satan has his biggest laugh in that so many are willing to blow themselves up in the name of a false prophet but so few are willing to sacrifice themselves daily in the name of the Lord Jesus Christ. Yes, Islam is the religion of submission, but it is not the religion of peace.

In order to identify the end-time Antichrist, look for the man of extreme rage supporting the beast of Islam. The mere presence of arrogance, pridefulness, and cunning is insufficient to identify the end-time Antichrist. Rather, extreme rage on par with that of Adolf Hitler (albeit more deftly hidden) will be the identifier. It is this person of rage who is the major threat to Israel as well as democracy. Just as Satan is enraged by God's Plan of Salvation and persecutes the people who belong to God (Revelation 12:17), so too will Satan's end-time Antichrist reflect that rage in his pursuit of God's people. Like Satan, the end-time Antichrist has nothing but contempt for all people of God. Nothing will appease his rage or mitigate his goal of exterminating all Jews and all Christians. However, the end-time Antichrist's rage will be so well-masked that most people will not perceive who he is. [*For example,* the venomous rage of Turkey's Erdogan is often carefully hidden.]

CHAPTER EIGHT

The Fullness of Time

The Holy Land was situated in the center of the ancient world, positioned in the center of the continents of Europe, Asia, and Africa — which three continents are homelands to all original races of the Earth. However, the Holy Land is central, not only to the world's most significant land masses and populations, but also to the world's most significant events: the birth, ministry, crucifixion, resurrection, ascension, and return of Christ Jesus.

To the God of the Holy Bible, *absolutely everything* in Earth's geography and history revolves around His Plan of Salvation through His *only-begotten* Son, Christ Jesus. Long before Christ Jesus was born, the God of the Holy Bible preordained the city of Bethlehem in the Holy Land — the city of Elimelech, Naomi, Ruth, Boaz, Obed, Jesse, and David — as the city of the Messiah's birth (Micah 5:2). And long before Christ Jesus was born, the God of the Holy Bible preordained the area of Megiddo in the Holy Land as the site for the final strategic battle that signals the forthcoming return of Christ Jesus (Revelation 16:16).

Christ Jesus was born in, lived in, ministered in, died in, was resurrected in, and ascended to Heaven from the Holy Land; and Christ Jesus returns to, and rules Earth from, the Holy Land. In effect, the Holy Land is the navel of this globe for the purpose of God's Plan of Salvation. Because of its importance to God's plan for our salvation, the Holy Land is also singularly important to Satan: In order to thwart God's Plan of Salvation and, thereby, circumvent his own demise, Satan has continually tried to annihilate God's chosen people, the Jews, as well as destroy the Holy Land, which belongs to the Jews.

(According to Satan's perverted thinking, if there are no Jews, then the return of Christ Jesus either will not happen at all or will be of null effect.)

Let us be reminded that the God of the Holy Bible gave the Holy Land in perpetuity to Abraham and his direct descendants through Isaac and Jacob, as recorded in Genesis 15:18, 26:3-4, and 35:12; Exodus 23:31; and Joshua 1:4. The original borders of the Holy Land included the Nile River to the south, Lebanon to the north, the Mediterranean Sea to the west, and the Euphrates River to the east. These borders constitute what the present author refers to as *Greater Israel* — in contrast to the smaller combined plots of land allotted to the tribes of Israel, as recorded in Numbers 34:3-14.

The natural boundaries and defenses around the land allotted to the tribes of Israel are the same as those surrounding the present-day nation of Israel. They include: (1) water to the west, (2) desert to the south, (3) the Jordan fissure (i.e., the Valley of Jordan) and desert to the east, and (4) mountains to the north. These natural boundaries and defenses were important, and still are important, in order to help isolate, seclude, and protect God's chosen people for their consecration to His service. To be sure, the Holy Land typifies the heavenly promised land, where the saints of God are eternally isolated, secluded, and protected from all pain and evil and eternally consecrated in service to Him. (Isolation, seclusion, protection, and consecration are all important parts in God's design for every individual Christian's life as well.)

In establishing the Holy Land, the God of the Holy Bible told the children of Israel many times not to form alliances or covenants with the pagan peoples who lived there (Exodus 23:32-33 and 34:12-15; Deuteronomy 7:2; Judges 2:2). Unfortunately, the children of Israel did not obey that command during ancient times, and they are not obeying that command in these end-times: In fact, under pressure from all nations of the world, the children of Israel will eventually allow the final end-time Antichrist to broker a seven-year peace treaty between them and the pagan people known as Palestinians (vis-à-vis

Hamas or its successor), which treaty the Antichrist will break after the first three-and-one-half years (Daniel 9:27), triggering the *Great Tribulation* as well as an outpouring of God's Wrath.

There will come a day, and that day is fast approaching, when the nation of Israel will be deserted by all other nations, including the United States and its allies, and attacked by its fiercest enemies, including the neighboring nation-states of Islam and their allies. Although no human being can deliver the children of Israel from these aggressors, the God of the Holy Bible can, and will, deliver them "when [the pagan foreigner] invades their land and marches into their borders" (Micah 5:6b KJV). Israel will be delivered by Christ Jesus himself!

> And the remnant of Jacob [i.e., the nation of Israel] shall be among the nations in the midst of many people as a lion among the beasts of the forest, as a young lion among the flocks of sheep. The lion will tread down and tear in pieces, and no one will be able to deliver [its aggressors] from the lion's hand.
> *Micah 5:8 KJV (Paraphrase)*

To be sure, through the return of Christ Jesus, the Lord God Almighty "will take vengeance in anger and wrath upon the nations that have not obeyed Him" (Micah 5:15 KJV Paraphrase). The Lord God Almighty will forever remain true to His word, promise, and oath concerning the nation of Israel:

> You, O Lord, will be true to Jacob [i.e., Israel], and demonstrate mercy to Abraham, as you pledged to our fathers long ago.
> *Micah 7:20 KJV (Paraphrase)*

The Holy Land continues to remain important because it figures prominently in the end-time events that have been preappointed, predetermined, and preordained according to the Lord God

Almighty's measures for *the fullness of time*.

> And he [the Angel Gabriel] said, "Look, I am making known to you what shall happen in the latter time of the indignation; for *at the appointed time the end shall be*."
> *Daniel 8:19 NKJV****

*** *NKJV* refers to citations from *Holy Bible New King James Version,* 1988, Thomas Nelson, Inc., Nashville, Tennessee. (All other Bible citations in this book are from the public domain King James Version of the Holy Bible.)

> And in the latter time of their kingdom, when the *transgressors have reached their fullness,* a king shall arise, having fierce features, who understands sinister schemes.
> *Daniel 8:23 NKJV*

> Both these kings' hearts shall be bent on evil, and they shall speak lies at the same table; but it shall not prosper, for the end will still be *at the appointed time.*
> *Daniel 11:27 NKJV*

> And some of those of understanding shall fall, to refine them, purge them, and make them white, until the time of the end; because it is still for *the appointed time.*
> *Daniel 11:35 NKJV*

> For the vision is yet for an *appointed time;* but at the end it will speak, and it will not lie. Though it tarries, wait for it; Because it will surely come, it will not tarry.
> *Habakkuk 2:3 NKJV*

{26} And He has made from one blood every nation of men to dwell on all the face of the earth, and has determined their *preappointed times* and the boundaries of their habitation, {27} so that they should seek the Lord, in the hope that they might grope for Him and find Him, though He is not far from each one of us; {28} for in Him we live and move and have our being, as also some of your own poets have said, "For we are also His offspring." {29} Therefore, since we are the offspring of God, we ought not to think that the Divine Nature is like gold or silver or stone, something shaped by art and man's devising. {30} Truly, these times of ignorance God overlooked, but now commands all people everywhere to repent, {31} because He has *appointed a day* on which He will judge the world in righteousness by the Man whom He has ordained. He has given assurance of this to all by raising him from the dead.

Acts 17:26-31 NKJV

For I do not desire, brothers and sisters, that you should be ignorant of this mystery, lest you should be wise in your own opinion, that hardening in part has happened to Israel until *the fullness of the Gentiles has come in*.

Romans 11:25 NKJV

But when the *fullness of the time* came, God sent forth His son, born of a woman, born under the Law [Torah], in order that he might redeem those who were under the Law, that we might receive the adoption of sons.

Galatians 4:4-5 NKJV

{7} In [Christ] we have redemption through his blood, the forgiveness of sins, according to the riches of [God's] grace {8} which He made to abound toward us in all wisdom and prudence, {9} having made known to us the mystery of His will, according to His good pleasure which He purposed in Himself, {10} that in the dispensation of *the fullness of the times* He might gather together in one all things in Christ, both which are in heaven and which are on earth in him, {11} in whom also we have obtained an inheritance, being predestined according to the purpose of Him who works all things according to the counsel of His will, {12} that we who first trusted in Christ should be to the praise of his glory.

Ephesians 1:7-12 NKJV

The concept of "fullness of time" is found in many places throughout Scripture. "Fullness of time" refers to: (1) the completion of a religious historic cycle or period, (2) a divinely-appointed epoch, and/or (3) a specific sequence of related religious and spiritual events in which there is an identifiable beginning and an identifiable end. Throughout Biblical history, God has predetermined times at which there is "fullness" (i.e., completion) — at which time a next "new beginning" occurs. "Fullness of time" is God's preordained *right time.*

For example, just before Jesus Christ ascended bodily into Heaven, he told his disciples to wait in Jerusalem until they were filled with "power from on high." That power was to come to them on the Day of Pentecost, fifty days after the bodily resurrection of Jesus Christ and ten days after his bodily ascension into Heaven. On that day, the Holy Spirit was given to all who believed — and, from then on, to all who would believe — on the crucified and risen Jesus as "the Christ," or *the Messiah,* and accept him as their personal Savior as well as the only Savior of the world. (This does not mean that everyone on Earth receives "eternal redemption" because, according to Scripture, those who consciously reject Jesus Christ as the *only-begotten* Son of God receive "eternal damnation.")

Today, in retrospect, it makes sense that God preordained the Day of Pentecost for a new beginning since the Day of Pentecost is a special Jewish Holy Day called *Shavuot.* The Day of Pentecost is the same day as the last day of the Jewish Feast of Weeks, also known as the "Feast of the Harvest" and the "Day of Firstfruits," described in Leviticus 23:5-21 and Deuteronomy 16:7-10. On the Day of Pentecost, the Ministry of Jesus Christ reaped a harvest of souls, who were the firstfruits of his public ministry after his death, burial, bodily resurrection, and bodily ascension to Heaven.

Many Christians celebrate the Day of Pentecost as the birthday of the Christian Church. Obviously, that day is significant in God's Calendar because He chose it as an important Holy Day for Jews as well as for Christians. In that Jesus Christ is the Head of the Church, and in that the "Head" can't really be separated from the "Body," the Church also had a very important beginning three and one-half years before the Day of Pentecost, when Jesus himself was baptized (that is, immersed in water) by John the Baptist ("Iohanan the Immerser") — at which time the Holy Spirit descended upon him as a dove (i.e., alighted on him in a manner similar to a dove).

Jesus began his public ministry after: (1) his immersion in water by John the Baptist; and (2) his immersion in the Holy Spirit by God the Father. Jesus was about thirty years old when these two events occurred (Luke 3:23).

In comparing seasons, Feasts, and Holy Days to one another in the Gospels and sequencing events in the Gospels according to them, it has been reasoned that the public ministry of Jesus Christ lasted for approximately three and one-half years — from the time of His full immersion in water and Spirit (i.e., his public anointing) until the time of his crucifixion.

It is clear in *The Gospel According to Matthew* that Herod the Great was alive at the time of the birth of Jesus Christ. Because recorded history teaches us that Herod the Great died in 4 B.C., and because he ordered the slaughter of all Hebrew males under the age of two, the probable year of the birth of Jesus Christ is no earlier than 6 B.C. and no later than 4 B.C.:

Then Herod, when he saw that he was deceived by the wise men, was exceedingly angry; and he sent forth and put to death all the male children who were in Bethlehem and in all its districts, from two years old and under, according to the time which he had determined from the wise men.
Matthew 2:16 NKJV

Based on events related to Herod the Great, one possible scenario is presented in Table Four:

YEAR	EVENT
4 B.C.	Christ Jesus is born in Bethlehem
27 B.C.	Christ Jesus begins his public ministry at the time of his baptism
30 B.C.	Crucifixion, bodily resurrection, and ascension of Christ Jesus
30 B.C.	Day of Pentecost signals birth of the Christian Church

Important Years in the Life of Christ Jesus

Table Four

Millennia (thousand year periods of time) are important to the Lord God Almighty. Scripture teaches us that "one day is as a thousand years" and "a thousand years is as one day" to Him (Psalm 90:4 KJV and 2 Peter 3:8 KJV). Sabbath-Day Millennialists believe that there are roughly six millennia (or "six days") before the millennium of peace (i.e., the "seventh day" of rest), which begins when Christ Jesus actually returns to Earth at the time of his "Second Coming" ("Second Advent") and rules for 1,000 years (as recorded in the Twentieth Chapter of the Book of Revelation). (For those who may conjecture otherwise, "Sabbath-Day Millennialism" is *not* a Christian denomination.)

According to this perspective, there are roughly 4,000 years from the appearance of Adam and Eve until the appearance of Jesus Christ (approximately four "days"), and there are approximately 2,000 years from the First Advent of Jesus Christ until his Second Advent (approximately two "days"). Thus (at the time that this book was written), we are soon nearing the time when "two days," or two millennia, will have passed since the time of Jesus Christ's public ministry on Earth (27 - 30 A.D.).

Using the dates of 27 A.D. and 30 A.D. and the "fullness of time" of 2,000 years, here are logical possibilities for the beginning and end of the seven-year Tribulation:

> 2020-2027 A.D.
> 2023-2030 A.D.
> 2027-2034 A.D.
> 2030-2037 A.D.

Prophetically-Relevant Calendar-Related Definitions

A *lunar year* of twelve cycles of moon phases is approximately 354 days long (29.5 days/lunar month x 12 lunar months = 354 days).

A *solar year* is the time from successive equinoxes (vernal or autumnal equinoxes) or successive solstices (summer or winter solstices), which is approximately 365.2425 days long. The phrase *solar year* describes the time that it takes the Earth to make one complete revolution around the Sun. (The Julian calendar, an earlier civil calendar, used a *solar year* of 365.25 days. The Gregorian calendar, our current civil calendar, uses a *solar year* at the more accurate measurement of 365.2425 days.)

An *equinox* is the time when the Sun crosses the equator, causing day and night on Earth to be of equal length (this occurs on or near March 21 for the Northern Hemisphere and on or near September 23 for the Southern Hemisphere).

A *solilunar year* (a *solunar* or *lunisolar year*) takes into consideration both lunar and solar events in order to measure time.

A *prophetical year* is the *solilunar year* used in various Bible prophecies as 360 days. Three hundred and sixty days is the approximate mean of a lunar year and solar year: $(354 + 365.25) \div 2 = 359.625 \approx 360$. (In mathematics, the symbol $\approx$ means *approximately.*)

Author's Notes: (1) It takes 33 solar years for the first day of the solar and lunar calendars to realign. (2) Jesus Christ was approximately 33 years old when he was crucified.

One Example of How the Bible Uses a Prophetic Year

As recorded in Daniel 9:24-27, the angel Gabriel explained to Daniel:

{24} Seventy weeks *(seventy sevens)* [70 *sevens* of years with each day representing one prophetical year = 490 prophetical years] are determined upon your people and upon your holy city [Jerusalem], to finish the transgression, and to make an end of sins, and to make reconciliation for iniquity, and to bring in everlasting righteousness, and to seal up *(ratify* or *complete)* the vision and prophecy, and to anoint the most Holy [Christ Jesus]. (italics and brackets mine)

{25} Know therefore and understand, that from the going forth of the commandment to restore and rebuild Jerusalem unto Messiah the Prince shall be seven weeks *(seven sevens)* [7 *sevens* of prophetical years with each day representing one year = 49 prophetical years], and threescore and two weeks *(sixty-two sevens)* [62 *sevens* of prophetical years with each day representing one year = 434 prophetical years]: the street shall be built again and the wall, even in troublous times. (italics and brackets mine)

{26} And after threescore and two weeks [at the end of the 483 prophetical years (49 prophetical years + 434 prophetical years = 483 prophetical years)] shall Messiah be cut off [slain/crucified], but not for himself: and the people of the prince that shall come [the final end-time Antichrist] will destroy the city and the sanctuary; and the end thereof will be with a flood, and unto the end of the war desolations are determined. (italics and brackets mine)

{27} And he ["the prince that shall come"] will confirm the covenant [treaty with Israel] with many for one week [seven years]: and in the midst [middle] of the week [after three-and-one-half years] he ["the prince that shall come"] will cause the sacrifice and the oblation [offering] to cease, and for the overspreading of abominations [idolatry] he ["the prince that shall come"] will make it desolate [with an idol on the Temple Mount], even until the consummation [end], and that determined shall be poured upon the desolate [in other words, God's appointed Wrath will destroy the idolaters at the end of the seven-year Tribulation]. (italics and brackets mine)

The 70 *sevens* of prophetical years in Daniel 9:24 represent 490 prophetical years. What are the events that begin the 490 prophetical years? Although no one knows for sure, many Bible scholars believe that the decree to rebuild the city of Jerusalem by first rebuilding its walls — given by the Persian King Artaxerxes Longimanus (Artaxerxes I) in the twentieth year of his reign in 445 B.C. (sometimes reported as 444 B.C.) and recorded in Chapter Two of Nehemiah — signals the beginning of the 490 prophetical years.

Author's Note: The Persian King Artaxerxes Longimanus (Artaxerxes I) was the grandson of King Darius I and the son of King Xerxes.

If the 69 *sevens* of prophetical years (483 prophetical years) given in Daniel 9:24-25 began in 445 B.C., then the 69 *sevens* of prophetical years (483 prophetical years) would end in approximately 34 A.D. (see *Calculation Box One*):

CALCULATION BOX ONE

Calculations to derive 34 A.D. require converting the 483 prophetical years given in Daniel 9:24-25 into days and then dividing the total number of days by 365.2425 (the number of days in a solar year):

483 prophetical years x 360 days/prophetical year = 173,880 days

173,880 days ÷ 364.2425 days/solar year = 477.3743 solar years

∴ 483 prophetical years ≈ 477.37 solar years
(∴ means *therefore* and ≈ means *approximately*)

445 B.C. + 477.37 solar years ≈ 34 A.D. (calculations follow)

444 solar years from 445 B.C. to 1 B.C.
+ 1 solar year from 1 B.C. to 1 A.D. (there is no zero A.D.)
+33 solar years from 1 A.D. to 34 A.D.
478 solar years ≈ 483 prophetical years

Although 34 AD is one of the possible years reported by Bible scholars for the crucifixion death of Christ Jesus, that year would only be true if our solar calendar were the perfectly accurate solar calendar described by the present author in the paragraph that follows:

The perfect solar calendar would give: (1) January 1, 1 A.D. as the birth date of Christ Jesus; (2) 30 A.D. as the year in which his ministry began; and (3) 34 A.D. as the year in which he was crucified (when he was approximately 33.5 years old).

However, in contradistinction to the perfect solar calendar envisioned by the present author, from the probable year of King Herod's death given earlier in this chapter, we know that Christ Jesus was born earlier than 1 A.D. Thus, based on Herod's death, Christ Jesus could have been born as early as 4 B.C. but no earlier than 6 B.C.

Many Bible scholars believe that there is a *fast forward,* or *gap,* of approximately 2,000 solar years from the time of the crucifixion of Christ Jesus (in Daniel 9:26) until the seven-year Tribulation (in Daniel 9:27), at the end of which Christ Jesus returns to Earth.

As the present author envisions it, the perfect solar calendar would have Christ Jesus return approximately 2,000 prophetical years *(two days* in the code language of Sabbath-Day Millennialism described earlier in this chapter) either (1) after his ministry began in 30 A.D. or (2) approximately 2,000 prophetical years after his crucifixion in 34 A.D. Calculations follow in Calculation Box Two:

CALCULATION BOX TWO

(2,000 prophetical years x 360 days/prophetical year) ÷ 364.2425 days/solar year
= 1,976.7051 solar years ≈ 1,977 solar years

∴ 2,000 prophetical years is approximately equal to 1,977 solar years

30 A.D. + 1,977 solar years = 2007 A.D.

34 A.D. + 1,977 solar years = 2011 A.D.

From the calculations given in Calculation Box Two, we must conclude that the timing for the return of Jesus Christ is *not* based on prophetical years (2007 A.D. and 2011 A.D. have already passed). Therefore, the only credible criterion we can use for the return of Christ Jesus is the seven-year Tribulation: We can only accurately conclude that Jesus Christ will return at the end of the seven-year Tribulation period given in Daniel 9:27.

Could the year that Christ Jesus returns be calculated on the basis of solar years? Using a solar calendar aligned with the dates given in Table Four, calculations for his possible return follow in Calculation Box Three:

> **CALCULATION BOX THREE**
>
> 27 A.D. + 2,000 solar years = 2027 A.D.
> (2,000 years after his ministry began)
>
> 30 A.D. + 2,000 solar years = 2030 A.D.
> (2,000 years after his crucifixion)

If Christ Jesus is to return in 2027 A.D., it would mean that the seven-year Tribulation *(the 70th seven of 490 prophetical years from 483 to 490 in Daniel 9:24-26, representing 7 prophetical years)* would begin in approximately 2020 A.D. And if Christ Jesus is to return in 2030 A.D., it would mean that the seven-year Tribulation *(the 70th seven of 490 prophetical years from 483 to 490 in Daniel 9:24-26, representing 7 prophetical years)* would begin in approximately 2023 A.D.

To be sure, we have a mathematical puzzle with regard to the exact length of the 2,000 year *gap,* or *fast forward. Perhaps* the only way to accurately know when the Tribulation begins is when the final end-time Antichrist signs a peace treaty with Israel. Because the present author believes that Iran is the nation to which the final end-time Antichrist belongs (as one of its citizens, as one of its appointed representatives, or as one of its multinational leaders), *perhaps* we will know the beginning of the seven-year Tribulation when Iran enters into a peace treaty with Israel. Because Iran will be in its ascendancy of power beginning in 2022/2023 A.D., *perhaps* Christ Jesus will return as soon as 2029/2030 A.D.

Author's Note: The present author was told from Heaven in February 2021 that "there will be 360 days of Persian ascendancy." He has interpreted this to mean that: (1) Iran will increasingly exert its power worldwide because of President Biden's weakness; (2) Iran's actual ascendant position of worldwide power begins in 2022/2023; (3)

Iran's treaty with Israel will be negotiated from Iran's position of economic power and military strength; and (4) the beginning year of Iran's ascendant position in 2022/2023, along with the signing of its treaty with Israel, starts the seven-year Tribulation.

Because the present author considers himself a Sabbath-Day Millennialist, he has used the possible timelines just presented as evidence to support the hypothesis that the time that we have before Jesus Christ will return to Earth is not only short but also measurable. (He is purposely *not* discussing the time of *the Rapture* in this work.) There are those who would say in response to these possible scenarios that "no one knows the hour and the day" of the return of Jesus Christ. It is agreed that Scripture tells us that we cannot know the hour or the day, but Scripture does not say that we cannot know the year or that we should not speculate about the year. What Christ Jesus said is:

> {32} Now learn this parable from the fig tree: When its branch has already become tender and puts forth leaves, you know that summer is near. {33} So when you see all these things [i.e., signs before the Second Coming], you will know that it is near, at the very doors. {34} Indeed, I say to you, this generation [i.e., *Age*] will by no means pass away till all these things are fulfilled. {35} Heaven and earth will pass away, but my words will by no means pass away. {36} But of that day and hour no one knows, no, not even the angels of heaven, but my Father only. [brackets mine]
>
> *Matthew 24:36 NKJV*

> Watch therefore, for you know neither the day nor the hour in which the Son of Man is coming.
>
> *Matthew 25:13 NKJV*

> But of that day and hour no one knows, neither the angels in heaven, nor the Son, but only the Father.
>
> *Mark 13:32 NKJV*

> It is not for you to know times or seasons which the Father has

put in His own authority.

Acts 1:7 NKJV

Although the present author does not know with absolute certainty when our Lord Jesus Christ will return, that does not mean that we should not, and cannot, reason when his return is likely as well as present the rationale for the likelihood of 2027 or 2030 A.D. for the purpose of discussion and debate in Christian circles concerning possibility, probability, and improbability.

Author's Notes on two possible scenarios:

Scenario #1: The interval of 30 A.D. to 2030 A.D. is an important period, or "fullness of time," because it marks the end of 2,000 years that can be called "The Church Age" (from the Day of Pentecost in 30 A.D. until Jesus Christ's possible return in 2030 A.D.).

Scenario #2: The interval of 27 A.D. to 2027 A.D. is another important period, or "fullness of time," because it marks the end of 2,000 years that can be called "The Messianic Period" (from the beginning of Jesus Christ's public ministry through its continuation by God's Holy Spirit until Jesus Christ's possible return in 2027 A.D.).

>>><<<

Regardless of whether Jesus Christ returns in 2027 or 2030 A.D. — or even 2060 A.D. (the year Sir Isaac Newton calculated that Jesus Christ would return) — every Christian should know with absolute certainty that Jesus Christ *will* return.

CHAPTER NINE
Human Conflict

On Friends and Enemies

In the tradition of the Old Testament, *friends* are *covenant partners* who signify their steadfast bond through an exchange or sharing of: (1) personal property (such as livestock, real estate, clothing, or weapons); (2) written or oral promises (such as oaths or vows); and/or (3) actions (such as shaking hands with one another or walking through the blood spilled between the split halves of an animal sacrifice).

In the tradition of the New Testament, *friends* are people whose covenant partnership has been established by their mutual acceptance of the shed blood of Jesus Christ for the remission of their sins and the cancellation of the debt they owe for their sins.

From one Biblical standpoint, people who are not New Testament friends can only be acquaintances or enemies to each other and to saved people. In this case, *acquaintances* are unsaved people who have not yet made an *informed,* conscious decision to accept or reject Jesus Christ as their personal Savior. From this perspective, acquaintances can only be prospective friends or prospective enemies to saved people. Acquaintances who make an *informed,* conscious decision to accept Jesus Christ as their personal Savior become New Testament friends to other saved people at the exact moment of their decision. (This does not mean that such individuals like each other's personalities and cultural values or have learned immediately to respect each other.) And acquaintances who make an *informed,* conscious decision to reject Jesus Christ as their personal Savior establish themselves as: (1) enemies of the God of the Holy Bible, (2) enemies of the Kingdom of the Creator-God, and (3) enemies of all people who belong to Jesus Christ. (This does not mean that such individuals are openly hostile or even discourteous to one another.)

Even if their rejection of Jesus Christ is not based on an *informed,* conscious decision, unsaved people are still among the enemies of the Creator-God, the Kingdom of God, and all people who belong to the Body of His Christ. Indeed, the Wrath (i.e., the Justified Anger) of the Creator-God still rests, or remains, on those who continue to reject Jesus Christ. Without God's Holy Spirit residing within them, evil can easily work through them. Although some learned values and mores may hinder evil from working through unsaved people, all human courtesies and customs can be conveniently discarded and ignored by unsaved people in favor of evil.

Even though the English word *enemy* has multiple meanings, the meaning that most closely fits its use in this book is: "a person or social group that is antagonistic to another person or social group, especially one seeking to injure, overthrow, or confound an identified opponent."

Because the first known use of the English word *enemy* was in the 13th century, the original writers of the Holy Bible did not have that word in mind when they used various Hebrew and Greek words that eventually would be translated into the English words *enemy* and *enemies.*

The Hebrew word *oyev* [H341], primarily translated as *enemy* in the King James Version of the Old Testament, means both "personal adversary" as well as "national adversary." The two primary Greek words that have been translated as *enemy/enemies* in different translations and versions of the New Testament are *echthros* [G2190] and *antidikos* [G476]. All three words are included in the following table (Table Five):

Strong's Number	Hebrew or Greek Word	Transliteration in Syllables	English Equivalents and Definitions
H341	אֹיֵב	ō·yāv′	1. personal adversary 2. national adversary
G2190	ἐχθρός	ekh-thros′	1. hostile human adversary 2. hostile demonic adversary 3. the Adversary (i.e., Satan or Devil)
G476	ἀντίδικος	än-tē′-dē-kos	1. hostile human adversary 2. hostile demonic adversary 3. the Adversary (i.e., Satan or Devil)

Table Five

As shown in the preceding table, the Greek words *echthros* and *antidikos* each have multiple meanings. At times, the two words are equivalent and, at other times, they are not. *For example,* both words can mean "hostile human adversary" and both words can refer specifically to Satan, who is "the Adversary" of the Creator-God. Thus, one really needs to see how each word is used in order to know what it means in its immediate Biblical context. (As a side note here, the word *echthros* and its variations and derivatives occur more frequently in the New Testament than the word *antidikos* and its variations and derivatives.)

Do Christians have human enemies?

There are those Christians who would cite Ephesians 6:12 to say that Christians do not have human enemies and that we should not think about other human beings as our enemies but as people in need of redemption (i.e., prospective Christians):

> For we wrestle not against flesh and blood, but against principalities, against powers, against the rulers of the darkness of this world, and against spiritual wickedness in high places.
> *Ephesians 6:12 KJV*

Unfortunately, Christians do not always counterbalance their understanding of Ephesians 6:12 with the recognition that the God of the Holy Bible permits murderous human conflict to exist and that the spiritual principalities and powers referenced in Ephesians 6:12 can, and do, work through human beings who have consciously yielded to evil. Out of cowardice and/or a superficial understanding of the Holy Bible, some people choose to pretend that murderous human conflict does not exist and that, because we have no real human enemies (according to their way of thinking), we should just give the problem to God by praying for His intervention and any ominous threats will eventually go away as we ignore them and think positively. They fail to recognize that some human beings have sold their souls to Satan and are beyond reclamation. Because evil is able to work through such people without constraint, these human beings are our enemies in addition to the demonic forces that are against us. In other words, Satan, his fallen angels, and all unclean spirits are our immortal enemies; and Muslims practicing Jihad are our mortal enemies (along with others who would also rob us of our personal freedoms). Indeed, whether they practice Jihad or not, all Muslims are called to Jihad by Allah in the Koran (al-Qur'an).

As a side note to Ephesians 6:12, some Christians take their literal understanding of that verse to such an extreme that they are unable to recognize that all human beings fight against their own flesh-and-blood hormones and neurotransmitters related to libido, addictions, and stress.

When Christ Jesus told us to love our human enemies (Matthew 5:44), he was, in fact, acknowledging that we have human enemies. Our real human enemies curse us, hate us, insult us, threaten us, persecute us, torture us, and murder us. Of course, Satan's demonic forces are linked to the actions of these human enemies. Consequently, we have human enemies not only toward whom we are to demonstrate love and forgiveness in response to Christ's command but also against whom we are to physically defend ourselves, our loved ones, and our respective nations and their allies from both external and internal threats.

When human beings consciously join forces with evil, they eventually become melded to evil — so much so that any humanity once existing in them cannot be found.

To say that Judeo-Christianity is not in the throes of a religious war with Islam during *the Pre-Millennium* is untrue *(the Pre-Millennium* is referring to the time that precedes the *Parousia,* or *arrival,* of Christ Jesus at his Second Coming). During *the Pre-Millennium,* all of Judeo-Christianity is at war with all of Islam, not a part or a portion of Islam but all of it.

You might ask: "Where in the Bible are wars between religions addressed?"

Wars between religions are certainly addressed in the Old Testament when the children of Israel were instructed to kill all of the inhabitants of the land of Canaan because the inhabitants were adherents of pagan religions. Killing them was intended to prevent eventual domination by the Canaanite pagans over the children of Israel through Canaanite physical aggression as well as intermarriage:

> You must kill all people that the Lord your God delivers to you. You must not have pity on them: neither shall you serve their gods because that will be a snare to you.
> *Deuteronomy 7:16 KJV (Paraphrase)*

> {5} And the children of Israel dwelt among the Canaanites, Hittites, Amorites, Perizzites, Hivites, and Jebusites: {6} they took their daughters to be their wives, and gave their daughters to their sons, and served their gods.
> *Judges 3:5-6 KJV (Paraphrase)*

Wars between religions are also addressed in the New Testament, specifically in the Book of Revelation: (1) World War III is essentially a religious war between the ideologies of Judeo-Christianity and Islam, culminating in the battle of Armageddon (Revelation 16:16) from the combined efforts of Muslims and non-Christian Gentiles to annihilate the Jews in Israel. And (2) World War IV at the end of the millennial reign of Christ Jesus on Earth — referred to as the "battle of Gog and Magog" in Revelation 20:8 — is also a war between the people who worship the God of the Holy Bible and those who worship His Adversary (i.e., Satan).

Although some Christians do not like using the word *religion,* the word *religion* in this book is simply referring to the practice of one's faith in the worship of what one assumes to be Deity. The word *religion* can also include the systematization of doctrines that are directly stated within and/or implied by the literature that forms the basis for one's faith and worship. (1) In his celebration of the liturgical ceremony of Passover, (2) in his participation of the other Jewish Feasts, and (3) in his honoring the annual pilgrimage to the Jerusalem Temple, Christ Jesus himself demonstrated that he was religious. But his religiosity was to a God-made, not man-made, religion. Indeed, some of the Jewish Feasts will also be celebrated during the Millennial Rule of Christ Jesus on Earth. (Also, in the Book of Revelation, Christ Jesus is described as dressed in the garb of the High Priest.) In other words, the word *religion* is not a bad word; it is the practice of one's religion that can be bad. In fact, the word *religion* is used quite positively in James 1:27 (KJV) relative to exercising one's faith in serving others in need.

To be sure, fighting physically in human conflict is a matter of conscience (hence the notion of the non-conscription of *pacifists* and *conscientious objectors* in various democracies during wartime). There are those who would say that a strict interpretation of the New Testament *requires* Christians to be pacifists and conscientious objectors. However, there are precedents for physical combat found in both the Old Testament and the New Testament in various human conflicts that have religion as their foundation. Of course, healthy debate is encouraged concerning whether Christians should physically fight in: (1) wars that are imperialistic, (2) wars that defend the borders of one's allies in addition to one's own borders, and (3) wars against foreign invaders and immigrants that seek to destroy from within the borders of one's country or the country of one's allies. It is healthy for Christians to debate among themselves concerning defensive tactics, including the use of so-called preemptive strikes against others whose imposing threats loom on the horizon.

The God of the Holy Bible does not contradict Himself. He states in Genesis 9:5-6:

> {5} "And surely for the shedding of your lifeblood I will require payment: from every beast I will require it as well as from man. From his fellow man I will require payment for the life of man. {6} Whichever person sheds the blood of man, by man shall his blood be shed, for God made man in His own image."
> *Genesis 9:5-6 KJV (Paraphrase)*

In the two previous verses, the God of the Holy Bible is stating clearly that He uses human beings to dispense at least some of His Wrath (i.e., His Justified Anger). Here, it would be helpful for Christians to remember that the God of the Holy Bible is not only the God of the New Testament but also the God of the Old Testament.

The Biblical principle of "an eye for an eye and a tooth for a tooth" is presented throughout the Old Testament. Yet Christ Jesus spoke against such human retribution and vengeance:

> {21} You have heard that it was said by those in the past, "You shall not murder; and whoever shall murder will be in danger of the final judgment [eternal damnation]:" {22} But I say to you, "Whoever is angry with his brother or sister without a cause shall be in danger of the final judgment: and whoever shall say to his brother or sister, 'Raca' [an Aramaic word that means *a senseless, empty-headed person*] shall be in danger of the council [i.e., Sanhedrin or overseeing body]: and whoever shall say, 'You fool,' shall be in danger of hell fire." [brackets mine]
> *Matthew 5:21-22 KJV (Paraphrase)*

Anger toward another human being "without a cause" (Matthew 5:22), especially toward a covenant partner in Christ Jesus, points in the direction of receiving the Creator-God's eternal damnation. In contrast, human conflict in response to provocation by an aggressor is understandable as well as acceptable to the God of the Holy Bible because the anger has a cause and is, therefore, justified.

To be sure, Christ Jesus did not say that we should not defend ourselves in like manner against those who would rob us of our human rights. The use of "in like manner" in the previous sentence is important. If those who oppose us try to use force against us, we are entitled to use force against them but only to defend ourselves and not to seek revenge. At the Garden in Gethsemane, the Apostle Peter was told to put down his sword in order to not interfere with the arrest of Christ Jesus. (It is noteworthy that the enemies of Christ Jesus were not there to slay his disciples.)

Do not misconstrue my "in like manner" comment in the previous paragraph to mean, *for example,* that if Jihadis (i.e., practicing Muslims) throw acid on your loved ones or set your loved ones on fire, then you should throw acid on them or set them on fire. No, you have a responsibility to protect yourself and others from the acid or fire (even if it takes the perpetrators' lives), but you do not have the right at some later date to throw acid on them or set them on fire. You do not have the right to act in a barbaric way even if someone intends to hurt or murder you or your loved ones in an act of barbarism. You only have the right to defend yourselves. If you end up inadvertently deflecting the acid toward them or throwing the fire back at them as you defend yourselves, then you have not committed an act of aggression or vengeance. However, you do not have the right to avenge the crime once it has already been committed unless you are convinced that other innocent people are in danger. And you do have the right to request that legal or military authorities arrest the culprits involved in any attacks against you or other innocent people in order to prosecute them.

You have the right to physically defend yourself and other people from attacks but never with a spirit of vengeance. Vengeance is not ours to dispense. Vengeance belongs to the God of the Holy Bible (Romans 12:19; Hebrews 10:30). However, we have not been asked by our Creator-God to abrogate our right to (1) physically defend ourselves or (2) make preparations to defend ourselves in the future.

>>>>><<<<<

On April 10, 2015, the present author posted the following comment on social media:

Christians should use whatever spiritual and physical means they have to defend themselves, their loved ones, and their nations against Jihadis. You do not need to start a conflict to finish it.

Following is the conversation that ensued between me and someone I will call "AV" (a native Indian living and working in Oman) as a result of my comment:

AV: *Pastor, does that mean we should take up arms in case of physical assault?*

ME: *Taking up arms is a matter of conscience for the individual. However, with that said, you can decide to not protect yourself because you are an adult and have that right, but you do not have the right to not protect your children because they are not mature enough in Christ Jesus to make the decision for themselves. So, my advice is for you to protect your vulnerable loved ones at the expense of your own life (for example, your aged parents, your wife, and your children and anyone else who lives in your home with you.) Why? "No greater love has any person than that they lay down their lives for their loved ones" (John 15:13 KJV Paraphrase).*

AV: *Pastor, defending at a cost of murdering someone is not right. In the Book of Acts, and during the early Christian persecution, they all trusted in God's intervention, not their own will and emotion. Please correct me if I'm wrong.*

ME: *AV, let us take this slowly. First, you are to discuss this with the Lord and follow His guidance. Second, indeed, you are to trust God and pray to Him for guidance and for His intervention. Third, if God chooses not to intervene, then you have the right to decide for yourself what you are going to do as a matter of conscience. Fourth, whatever you decide for yourself does not apply to your children.* **YOU ARE TO PROTECT THEM WITH YOUR VERY LIFE.** *You do not have the right to sacrifice your children. You have the right to become a martyr for the Christian faith, but you do not have the right to decide for your children if they are to become martyrs. Fifth, there is a difference between "murdering" someone and defending yourself physically. Nowhere have I asked you to murder anyone. And, to be sure, you can defend yourself physically without intending to take someone's life if that is a matter of conscience for you.*

ME: *Christ Jesus states in Mark 5:22: "But I say to you, 'Whoever is angry with his brother WITHOUT A CAUSE shall be in danger of the final judgment: and whoever shall say to his brother "Raca" (an Aramaic word that means "a senseless, empty-headed person") shall be in danger of the council: and whoever shall say "You fool" shall be in danger of hell fire."' If someone is trying to murder you or your family, THAT IS A JUST CAUSE to be angry and, also, a just cause to protect yourself and your family in physical self-defense.*

ME: *"Murder" means to take someone's life without a sufficient reason or just cause. Defending yourself is NOT murder.*

AV: *Pastor, then why was this not practiced by the first Christians and 1st century believers during their persecution?*

ME: *Throughout the past 2,000 years, there have been many Christians who have defended their homes, their loved ones, and their* nations. *If it were not for Christians fighting against the Nazis during World War II, the world would have been in great darkness for the past 70 years. These courageous and honorable men and women gave their lives so that I and my family might live in safety. Turning your cheek for a second slap is not the same as permitting your children to be raped or beheaded.*

AV: *Pastor, I accept the fact that no dad would just sit hopeless and cry while his daughters are raped and his sons are beheaded in front of him. A dad would do anything to defend his children and family. But I believe that the dad's action is more out of emotion and it would be automatic rather than a thought and then action. These cases could not be taken as a doctrine but must be justified on a case-to-case basis.*

ME: *There is no case-to-case basis when protecting your children from rape or beheading. Anger is justifiable when there is a just cause. The intended rape or beheading of your children is a justifiable cause for anger. Even Jesus got angry.*

AV: *I accept, Pastor, that we will have to do something in such cases.*

ME: *I am proud of you that you would lay down your life for your family and friends.*

AV: *Any dad or son would do whatever he can to defend his family and friends. No man would sit and murmur "Vengeance belongs to the Lord" (Romans 12:19) when a knife is on his wife's neck.*

ME: *Amen. Always take courage in our Lord. AV, one last thought here: Defending yourself is not vengeance. Vengeance seeks to take control, pay back, and punish. Defense seeks to protect.*

AV: *True, normally, we Christians when persecuted have this verse [i.e., Romans 12:19] quoted from the Bible, and we tend to believe in heart that God has put us through this persecution and that He will repay.*

ME: *Amen, we are not to exact payment for anyone else's sins against us, but we may defend ourselves.*

AV: *True, I accept what you mean.*

ME: *I am glad that we had this discussion.*

AV: *Me too, Pastor, I started thinking with a new perspective after we spoke. Thank you, God bless.*

At this juncture, it is important to again quote Romans 12:19 along with the verse that precedes it:

{18} IF IT IS POSSIBLE, and as much as it depends on you, live peaceably with all people. {19} Dearly beloved, avenge not yourselves, but rather give place to God's Wrath because it is written, "Vengeance is mine; I will repay," says the Lord [from Deuteronomy 32:35, 32:41, 32:43]. [emphasis and brackets mine]
Romans 12:18-19 KJV (Paraphrase)

Reinforcing what was previously quoted from Genesis 9:5-6, it is equally important to note that sometimes the Lord uses human beings to dispense His vengeance:

"And I will lay My vengeance upon Edom by the hand of My people Israel: and they shall do in Edom according to My anger and according to My fury. And they [the people of Edom] shall know My vengeance," says the Lord GOD. [brackets mine]
Ezekiel 25:14 KJV (Paraphrase)

On Repentance and Forgiveness

A *Jihadi, Jihadist,* or *Mujahid* (all three words are synonymous) is a practicing Muslim who acts in violent or non-violent ways to defend his faith and spread its views regardless of the cost to his own life or to the lives of non-Muslims. The foundations for Jihad (i.e., the so-called *holy war* or *holy struggle*) are found throughout the Koran (al-Qur'an). Jihad is the religious duty of every Muslim and, although truces, pacts, and ceasefires with non-Muslims may be agreed upon, they will always be temporary: There can be no lasting peace between Muslims and non-Muslims because Muslims subscribe to the tenets of deception to further their cause (i.e., *taqiyya, idtirar, kitman,* and *hiyal*).

A careful reading of Scripture shows that, although the God of the Holy Bible hates all sin, He hates most: (1) the worship of false gods, (2) the spilling of innocent blood, and (3) blasphemy. When combined, these three actions especially incur God's Justified Anger. During the Tribulation, God's Wrath is dispensed upon all who do not repent of worshiping false gods, shedding innocent blood, and blaspheming Him. The worst of God's Wrath is especially poured out on those who shed innocent blood in the blasphemous worship of the false god Allah.

Without repentance there is no forgiveness of sins for any unsaved sinner. Therefore, unless messages of forgiveness from Christians to Jihadis include a clear call to repentance, those messages fall short. Without calling Jihadis to repentance, messages to them of love and forgiveness imply universal salvation (i.e., everyone is saved regardless if they repent or not). All messages on love and forgiveness to Jihadis should be *blood messages* conveying that all blood shed by Jihadis and Christian martyrs cannot equal the power of the shed blood of Jesus Christ. Without the shedding of Christ's blood, there can be no forgiveness of sins (see Hebrews 9:22). In order for Jihadis to receive salvation, they must learn that when innocent blood is spilled, the blood of the perpetrator (i.e., the murderer) is actually *required* by the God of the Holy Bible unless the sins of the perpetrator are covered, cancelled, and remitted by the substitutionary offering of the shed blood of Jesus Christ in conjunction with: (1) the personal acceptance of Jesus Christ as Lord and Savior and (2) repentance by the perpetrator.

If you, the reader, desire salvation, I invite you to believe in your heart and confess with your mouth by repeating the following prayer out loud:

Dear Lord Jesus, I ask that you forgive me of my sins. I am sorry for them and I repent of them. I accept you as my Lord and Savior. I know that you are the only-begotten Son of the one true and only real Creator-God, the God of the Holy Bible. I invite you into my soul, my heart, and my mind, and I ask that you help me to live for you each day. Thank you for hearing my prayer, for accepting me as one of your own, and for cleansing me of all of my sins by your shed blood. Dear Jesus, help me to trust in you alone throughout the rest of my life.

APPENDIX A

Comparison Chart		
Except for the reverse order spelling, Arabic and Hebrew are written right to left.		
Word	Letters	Explanation
محمد	dal-mem-he-mem	Arabic Spelling of Mohammed/Muhammad (no vowels)
מחמד	dalet-mem-chet-mem	Common Hebrew Transliteration (no vowels)
מהמד	dalet-mem-hey-mem	Alternate Hebrew Transliteration (no vowels)
מוחמד	dalet-mem-chet-waw-mem	Common Hebrew Transliteration
מוהמד	dalet-mem-hey-waw-mem	Alternate Hebrew Transliteration
מוהאמיד	dalet-yod-mem-aleph-hey-waw-mem	Correct Order Transliteration (cryptographic spelling)
דימאהום	mem(final)-waw-hey-aleph-mem-yod-dalet	Reverse Order Transliteration (cryptographic spelling)

Transliterations for Mohammed

Table Six

Answers to Possible Questions about "666"

1. In the chapter entitled "How It All Adds Up" (Chapter Four), I give the transliterated Hebrew spelling of the name *Mohammed* in Table One. How can I explain this transliteration when the modern Hebrew version of the name has no Yod (Yud)?

Although there is no Yod in the modern Hebrew version of the name, that is not to say that the name seen by the Apostle John in his vision circa 95 AD, and recorded cryptographically as "666" in Revelation 13:18, did not have a Yod in it. Because the written alphabet letter Yod has varying vowel qualities, at times it may be phonetically pronounced somewhat similar to a "long" English e (accent macron) [as used in the plural form of Hebrew masculine nouns] and, at other times, like a "short" English e (accent breve). (In addition to Yod having vowel qualities, it can even have consonantal qualities or be quiescent [silent].)

To be sure, the subscript vowel points used as vowel cues in modern Hebrew were not used by ancient Hebrew scribes and copyists. Hence, it is reasonable and defensible to include Yod as the sixth Hebrew alphabet character in "Mohamed." Because the name "Mohamed" did not originate in ancient Hebrew, modern Hebrew cannot claim to accurately represent its purest written form (nor, for that matter, can modern Hebrew accurately reproduce all sounds associated with the ancient Yod and its various dialectical and regional forms). Moreover, modern transliterators do not always do a good job: just think of how horribly far the modern English pronunciation *Solomon* is from the ancient Hebrew *Shlomo*. In conclusion, it is no small coincidence that the Hebrew letter Yod is related to the Greek vowel Iota (I, i), both having originated from the Phoenician Yod.

2. Mem usually has a value of 40 associated with it. Why have I assigned a value of 600 to it?

First, what I list as having a value of 600 is a final Mem, not an initial or "mid-word" (i.e., medial) Mem, which always has a value of 40. When I lived in Chicago some years ago, I researched this in the Asher Library at the Spertus Institute of Jewish Studies. There, I found a Kabbalistic (Qabbalistic or Cabbalistic) precedence for assigning a numerical value of 600 to a final Mem. This is further substantiated in *Kabbalah* by Charles Ponce (Quest Books, Wheaton, 1978, page 33, ISBN 0-8356-0510-8), which, incidentally, I purchased at Spertus. Note: For those Christians who have been taught to avoid Kabbalism, please know that the use of Hebrew characters for numbers is a common practice in Hebrew and that the practice originated independently of Kabbalism.

3. Why do I have the name *Mohammed* written backwards?

It is my belief that the name *Mohammed* was given to the Apostle John in cryptographic form (i.e., "hidden writing"). Writing backwards (which is to say, writing letters in reverse order) has long been a way to mask or hide words and messages from casual observers, which was the intent of the Holy Spirit in the identification of the name that is numerically represented as "666" in the Book of Revelation.

The blasphemy that Jesus Christ (Y'shua H'Moshiach) is not God's *only-begotten* Son carries with it a self-imposed curse. Because the name *Mohammed* is perpetually unholy and, thus, has an eternal curse connected to it, God's Holy Spirit chose not to "speak" or directly convey that name to the Apostle John other than cryptographically (that is, in reverse order using a mathematical cipher). Because the word *Mohammed* represents unmitigated evil, the Holy Spirit will not use or speak of that word except in a cryptographic way: The Holy Spirit is too pure and too holy to use or speak of that word except in the cryptographic way it is used in Revelation 13:18.

4. Does it make a difference in Hebrew or Jewish numerology if the Hebrew form of the word is transliterated from the English spellings "Mohammed" וֹ or "Muhammad" וּ ?

No, although there is a phonemic, or sound, difference between the "long o" sound (accent macron, as in "Mohammed") and the "oo" sound (diphthong "oo," as in "Muhammad"), there would be no numerological difference between the Hebrew transliterated forms of "Mohammed" and "Muhammad" (provided, of course, that the "vav" or "waw" is still there). To be sure, the modern Hebrew form of the word, regardless of English transliteration (or Hebrew transliteration, for that matter), is still written with a "vav" or "waw." That there is a difference in vowel points between the "long o" and "oo" phonemes in Hebrew does not change the numeric value of the grapheme so cued (in this case, "vav"). More specifically, although the vowel point "cholem" would be used in the transliterated form of "Mohammed" and the vowel point "shuwreq" would be used in the transliterated form of "Muhammad," the indicated "vav" or "waw" is present either way and would still have the numeric value of 6 (six). As an additional note, "vav" is used as a vowel in the spelling of "Mohammed" in the same way that "vav" is used as a vowel in the Hebrew spelling of *dode/dodah (uncle/aunt)* [H1730/H1733] in *Strong's Exhaustive Concordance of the Bible*].

5. What about the double letter "m" representation in *Mohammed?* Does this require that a double grapheme "mem" be used when that word is transliterated from English to Hebrew?

No, the use of double letters in English or other languages that use the Roman alphabet was instituted more as a convenience for lexicographers, compositors, publishers, and linguists who desired convenience in dividing words by syllables and/or who wanted to emphasize that a particular sound was sustained as a bridge between two vowel-based syllables (syllables are always vowel-based irrespective of the presence or absence of a written vowel grapheme or vowel point).

6. Is the name *Mohammed* found anywhere in the Holy Bible?

No, except for the cryptographic representation of *Mohammed* as "666" in Revelation 13:18, the name *Mohammed* does not occur anywhere in the Holy Bible.

Some Muslims literate in Hebrew claim that the presence in the Bible of the Hebrew words *machmad* (singular) and *machmadim* (plural) [H4261 in *Strong's Exhaustive Concordance of the Bible*] is evidence that the name *Mohammed* is used in the Bible.

Strong's Number	Hebrew Singular	Hebrew Plural
H4261	מַחְמָד	מַחֲמַדִּים

Table Seven

As a point of information, the Hebrew words *machmad* and *machmadim* — translated in the Bible as *beloved, delightful, desired, desirable, goodly, lovely, pleasant,* and *pleasant thing* — are found in the following thirteen verses of the Bible: 1 Kings 20:6; 2 Chronicles 36:19; Song of Solomon 5:16; Isaiah 64:11; Lamentations 1:10, 1:11, 2:4; Ezekiel 24:16, 24:21, 24:25; Hosea 9:6, 9:16; and Joel 3:5.

However, because the Hebrew word *machmad* provides an inaccurate transliteration of the word *Mohammed, machmad* should never be used to prove that the name *Mohammed* is in the Bible. Unfortunately, some of the confusion originates from one common, albeit inaccurate, Hebrew transliteration for *Mohammed* that uses a "chet" instead of a "hey" when "hey" offers the more accurate transliteration of *Mohammed* from Arabic. [Listen to the word spoken in Arabic; it has a soft "hey" sound and not a hard "chet" sound.] Paradoxically, when modern Israeli newspapers have transliterated the name of the American boxer *Mohammed Ali* into Hebrew, they use a "hey" and not a "chet."

APPENDIX B

The Seven Feasts of Israel

The present author acknowledges that alternate methods exist for calculating a few of the dates indicated in the table on the next page (Table Eight).

All Seven Feasts in Table Eight were established by the God of the Holy Bible not only for the sanctification of Israel but also to signal the sequence of end-time events.

The Hebrew years 5784 and 5785 and A.D. 2024 in Table Eight are used only as templates for comparing other years.

Feast Name	Duration	Hebrew Religious Calendar	Scriptural References	Fulfillment √ = already fulfilled
Passover (Commemorates 10th Plague of Egypt)	1 Day (8 Days)	1st month 14th day 14 Nissan 5784 (Monday at Sundown: April 22, 2024)	Leviticus 23:4-6 Exodus 12:1-46 Mark 11 John 19:31-36 Joshua 5:10-12 Matt. 26:19-20; 26-30 John 1:29 1 Corinthians 5:7	The Shed Blood of Jesus Christ as our Passover Lamb (His Shed Blood commemorated by "the fruit of the vine" in Communion) √
Unleavened Bread (Commemorates flight from Egypt)	7 Days	1st month 15th –21st days 15-21 Nissan 5784 (Tuesday, April 23 to Monday, April 29, 2024)	Exo.12:15-20; 34; 39 Leviticus 23:5-8 1 Corinthians 5:7-8 Matthew 16:6 Mark 8:15 Psalm 16:10 Acts 2:22-31 Acts 13:34-37	Sinless Life of Jesus Christ and His Body Incorruptible in Death during Burial (His Broken Body commemorated by broken bread in Communion) √
First Fruits -occurs in Spring-	1 Day (1st Sunday in Feast of Unleavened Bread)	1st month 19 Nissan 5784 (Sunday, April 28, 2024)	Leviticus 23:10-11 Proverbs 3:9-10 Matthew 27:1,6 1 Corin. 15:12-23 1 Thess. 4:16-17 Matthew 27:53	Bodily Resurrection of Jesus Christ √
Harvest (Weeks) (Latter First Fruits) (Commemorates giving of 10 Commandments) -occurs in Summer-	1 Day (7th Sunday after the Feast of First Fruits)	3rd month 9 Sivan 5784 (Sunday, June 16, 2024)	Leviticus 23:15-22 Acts 1:1-1:13; 2:1-22 Deuteronomy 16:9-10	Pentecost (Birth of the Church by the Holy Spirit) √
Trumpets (Rosh Hashanah) First day of Jewish civil new year	1 Day (1st Day of the Seventh Month)	7th month 1 Tishrei 5785 (Wednesday at Sundown: October 2, 2024)	Leviticus 23:23-25 Numbers 29:1 Joshua 6:2-5 1 Thess. 4:16-17 1 Corin. 15:51-54	Rapture of Church (First step of a two-step Parousia) Not Yet Fulfilled
Atonement (Yom Kippur)	1 Day (10th Day of the Seventh Month)	7th month 10 Tishrei 5785 (Friday at Sundown: October 11, 2024)	Leviticus 16:1-34; 23:26-30 Zechariah 12:10; 13:1,6 Romans 11:26	2nd Coming (Advent) of Jesus Christ to deliver all Israel (Second step of a two-step Parousia) Not Yet Fulfilled
Tabernacles (Shelters) (Sukkot)	7 Days (15th - 21st Day of the Seventh Month)	7th month 15-21 Tishrei 5785 (Starts Wed. at Sundown: October 16-23, 2024)	Leviticus 23:34-43 Zech. 8:3; 14:9,16-19 Ezekiel 37:26-27	Millennial Rule of Jesus Christ on Earth Not Yet Fulfilled

The Seven Feasts of Israel

Table Eight

APPENDIX C
Assumptions and Recommendations

What to remember when interacting with Muslims:

1. True academic dialogue is only possible between a Christian and a Muslim when both participants have read the entire Koran (al-Qur'an) and the entire Holy Bible. If not, then true academic dialogue is not possible between them. This makes such dialogue impossible for those Muslims who have not read the entire Holy Bible and for those Christians who have not read the entire Koran (al-Qur'an). (*True academic dialogue* is defined here as "objective, educated debate" that may involve refutational and nonrefutational references to the written documents that are the foundation for one's personal belief system as well as for understanding the basis for another's personal belief system.) Obviously, Christians and Muslims may communicate with one another without using academic dialogue, but, in that case, they would have to speak to each other about spiritual concepts and testify about personal convictions and personal experiences, which can only be subjective because of their dependence on the "personal." To be sure, without heartfelt personal testimony about life-changing faith in Jesus Christ, and without love in our hearts for all others, including Muslims, true academic dialogue can fall into the abyss of intellectual exercise.

2. It is important for Christians in Western countries to remember that illiteracy rates are very high in some Islamic nations. Illiteracy rates

are especially high (between 75 and 25 per cent) in the following Islamic countries, which are listed in their descending order: Afghanistan, Pakistan, Mauritania, Morocco, Yemen, Sudan, Djibouti, Algeria, Egypt, Iraq, and Tunisia.

3. The god of the Koran (al-Qur'an) is simply not the same as the God of the Holy Bible. The Koran was inspired by the spirit of Antichrist through the false prophet Mohammed and was written by that one person, and that one person alone. The Holy Bible was inspired by God's Holy Spirit and was written by many people; and the continuity of its message and complementarity of its individual writings attest to its divine authorship and authority. *Continuity* and *complementarity* here are provided: (a) through the Biblical genealogies from Adam to Jesus Christ; (b) through Biblical prophecies related to the Advent of the Jewish Messiah (the First Coming of Jesus Christ); (c) through the fulfillment of that Advent in Jesus Christ (who is both "the *only-begotten* Son of God" and "God Incarnate"); (d) through teachings that demonstrate that God requires an unblemished blood sacrifice for the forgiveness of sins; and (e) through the only possible fulfillment of that requirement in the crucifixion of Jesus Christ.

4. Although the Arabic word *Allah* is not an evil word (it means "the god" in Arabic), the word *Allah* represents evil because it represents: (a) the spirit of Antichrist, (b) Satan, and (c) a false god (i.e., a pagan god). *Allah* represents the god of the Koran (al-Qur'an) and not the one true and only real Creator-God, the God of the Holy Bible. Therefore, use of the word *Allah* by Jews and Christians should be discouraged because *Allah* does not represent the God of the Holy Bible. It gives the hearer or reader the wrong impression that the god of the Koran (al-Qur'an) is the God of the Holy Bible when it is not. Similarly, in the Old Testament, the word *Baal* was often used for a specific false god. Although the Hebrew word *Baal* is not an evil word (it means "lord" in Hebrew), the word *Baal* represents: (a) evil, (b) Satan, and (c) a false god (i.e., a pagan god) and, therefore, would never be used in isolation as a name for the God of the Holy Bible. The same is true for *Allah*. *Allah* is a pseudonym for *Satan*.

5. Christians in Islamic countries should (a) use expressions in their native language that mean "Heavenly Father" or (b) simply say "the God of the Holy Bible" to make sure that the reader or listener knows that they are not speaking about the god of the Koran (al-Qur'an). Christians should also be encouraged to use the expressions "the *only-begotten* Son of God," "the Savior," and "the Lord Jesus" (see Table Three) when speaking about Jesus Christ to non-Christians.

6. Many, if not most, Muslims understand the concept underlying the blood sacrifice of animals. Therefore, it is possible to use this practice to help explain the role of Jesus Christ as the Lamb of God (i.e., the only sacrifice acceptable to God because of his unblemished life as the *only-begotten* Son of God, who, though tempted to sin, did not sin).

7. Muslims believe: (a) that God does not have an *only-begotten* Son, (b) that God does not need to have an *only-begotten* Son, and (c) that it is blasphemy to say that God has an *only-begotten* Son. Muslims believe that we are all children of *Allah* and, therefore, are all "sons." Christians can minister to Muslims by talking about the necessity for the Creator-God to have an *only-begotten* Son as an unblemished sacrifice to bear the sins of the world (i.e., our own individual sins, collectively).

8. All authentic Christians believe in one God. The titles "God the Father," "God the Son," and "God the Holy Spirit" sometimes confuse Muslims and cause them to conclude that Christians believe in three gods, which is simply not true. All authentic Christians believe in one God only, the God of the Holy Bible. Paradoxically, some authentic Christians think that other authentic Christians believe in three Gods. However, ignorance, not malice, bears the burden for their erroneous conclusion. Muslims think they believe in the same deity in whom Christians believe, and even call upon their descent from Abraham to help prove their claim. However, the god of Islam is a different god from the Lord God Almighty. *Allah* is not *Yahweh*. The god of the Koran (al-Qur'an) is Satan, the eternal Adversary of the God of the Holy Bible.

9. Muslims are taught that the Bible has been corrupted, but that is not true. There are enough copies of Old Testament books that have survived from Qumran (i.e., the Dead Sea Scrolls) from thousands of years ago to attest to the accuracy of the Old Testament text that we possess today, and there are enough ancient manuscripts of the New Testament that have survived to attest to its authentic status as well. Muslims point to the fictitious work known as "The Gospel of Barnabas" as authentic Scripture, when it is not. There is no historical or factual basis for such a claim. Although a pseudepigraphal work known as "The Epistle of Barnabas" exists, it is not "The Gospel of Barnabas."

10. Christians can minister to Muslims by emphasizing God's grace and mercy to sinners who have confessed their sins and believe on the Lord Jesus Christ (i.e., believe in his crucifixion as the only sacrifice acceptable to God for the forgiveness of sins). "On" is used here in contrast to "in" because, *for example,* although Mohammed actually lived and, therefore, I believe "in" him (i.e., in his existence), I do not stake my eternal salvation on that belief nor do I daily trust him to lead and guide me. Christians trust in the Lord Jesus Christ to guide them through God's Holy Spirit, (a) who has been deposited within their souls as an assurance of their eternal salvation and the future redemption of their bodies, and (b) who currently uses their individual bodies as a "tabernacle," or dwelling-place.

11. Because Muslims do not have the Holy Spirit indwelling them (even if they are polite, kind, and courteous), they can only understand Christ and Christianity if God grants them repentance through the knowledge of salvation by the shed blood of Jesus Christ for the forgiveness of their sins. Christians should pray for God to grant Muslims repentance of their sins and knowledge of salvation at the same time that they pray to the God of the Holy Bible to lead them (the Christians) in terms of what they are to say, how they are to say it, and when they are to say it. Christians should recognize that some Muslims are only Muslims because they have been indoctrinated into that belief system from childhood and that they have not technically

given their lives completely over to Satan yet by exercising a free will choice. I write "yet" because they will end up giving their lives completely to Satan if they refuse to listen to — and refuse to understand — the gospel of salvation through Jesus Christ, and Jesus Christ alone.

12. A Christian should not use statements in the Koran (al-Qur'an) seemingly supportive of Christ Jesus, Christians, Christianity, Moses, Jews, Judaism, or the Prophets of the Old Testament (i.e., the Hebrew Tanakh) to help evangelize Muslims (i.e., minister to Muslims the gospel of salvation through Jesus Christ and Jesus Christ alone) other than those statements which attest to the actual existence of the people just mentioned. Likewise, a Christian should not use statements from the Koran (al-Qur'an) that are seemingly compatible with truths found within the Bible. Overall, such approaches only lend credibility to the claim that the Koran (al-Qur'an) is Holy Scripture when it is not. Such statements help legitimize the Muslim's view that the Koran (al-Qur'an) was authored by the one true and only real God — known to Jews as *Yahweh, Yehowah,* or *Yehovah* (the Self-Existent One and LORD of the Universe) and known to Christians as Y'shua H'Moshiach (Jesus the Messiah, or Jesus the Christ), the *only-begotten Son of God* as well as *God in flesh.*

13. The wrath of God (i.e., His Justified Anger) is not the same as the cruelty of Satan. Satan terrorizes humanity through the fear of threats to one's physical, emotional, and spiritual well-being. *For example:* (a) Satan terrorizes through the fear he causes by accusing and re-accusing Christians of their sins against God; that these sins have not been forgiven by God even if they have been confessed; and that individuals are eternally separated from the Creator because of their sins. (b) By controlling the global economic world system, Satan terrorizes through the fear engendered in people that they will continue to do without necessities or that they will one day no longer have the privileges they now enjoy. (c) Satan terrorizes Christians through physical illness and through threats of physical death and murder. (This is not to say that some forms of physical disability are not

sanctioned, permitted, or even given by God or that God has not permitted some Christians to be martyred for their faith.) (d) Satan terrorizes people by creating chaos to rob them of their peace and joy. Satan is the god of destruction, desolation, and war through terrorism.

14. Christians may try to witness to Muslims through benevolent humanitarianism provided that, at the same time, they also introduce the gospel message of salvation through Jesus Christ and Jesus Christ alone. Without an introduction to this gospel, all "good" deeds are "without faith," bringing honor, glory, and praise to the doer but not to the God of the Holy Bible. However, although Christians should try to sow the seed of the gospel message of Jesus Christ to Muslims, Christians must not cast their pearls before swine and Christians must abandon Muslims when Muslims are openly inhospitable to the gospel message of Jesus as the *only-begotten* Son of the God of the Holy Bible and Savior of the world. (Jesus said to shake the dust from off your feet when people refuse to receive the gospel message of salvation.)

15. To the best of their ability, Christians should not try to incite Muslims to violence or acts of revenge in order (a) to prove their point that the god of Islam is a god of war through terrorism or (b) to prove that they are good Christians by seeking martyrdom for themselves. Although true Christian martyrdom exists, we are not to seek martyrdom for ourselves; however, we may choose to sacrifice ourselves to honor God and/or to help protect others.

16. Christians should not seek martyrdom because martyrdom is ordained by God and not by mortals. The savage beheading of Christians by Muslims has happened and will continue to happen, and Christians should accept such a fate if they find themselves in such a position without recourse, but Christians should not purposely place themselves in harm's way in order to receive a greater reward in Heaven. Such attempts are designed to serve themselves and not God. To be sure, however, it is not self-serving to declare that one is

unafraid of being murdered for his or her faith in Jesus Christ as the *only-begotten* Son of God and one's personal Savior.

17. Christians should assume that learning how to minister to Muslims is a gradual process and that they will make many mistakes along the way, especially if they rely on their own ignorance, pride, and willfulness. They need to learn from their own mistakes, asking for God's forgiveness and direction along the way, in order to move forward and become more effective witnesses. Effective witnessing begins with the love of Christ Jesus for all people, including Muslims.

18. Pray that God grants repentance to Muslims by imparting the knowledge of salvation through Jesus Christ and Jesus Christ alone. Especially pray for those Muslims who have been indoctrinated into their belief system since childhood and have not had an opportunity to make a free will decision as to where to place their individual faith. Pray that God reveal the source of the Muslim faith to Muslims as well as to Christians. Pray that God reveal the source of the Christian faith (i.e., the crucified, resurrected, ascended, and returning Christ Jesus) to Muslims as well as to nominal, or secular, Christians.

19. Read aloud the Gospel of John and the Book of Acts to Muslims.

20. Emphasize that the God of the Holy Bible is the God of love and not the god of war through terrorism. Explain the difference between God's righteous judgment through wrath (or divine judgment) as opposed to Satan's cruelty through fear and intimidation. Acknowledge that, historically, both Christians and Muslims have been guilty of terrorism, vengefulness, and attempting to convert one another through force (a real conversion is an exercise of one's free will and never coerced).

21. Emphasize how easily one person can distort who and what God is. That the entire Koran (al-Qur'an) was written by one person automatically puts it into a suspicious category as opposed to the Holy

Bible, which was written by many people and, yet, has significant unity, continuity, and complementarity throughout.

22. Emphasize that the Holy Bible is not a work that has been corrupted by human beings over thousands of years. The roles of the ancient Hebrew "lawyers" (Torah scholars) and "scribes" (Tanakh copyists) helped to ensure that the Old Testament was painstakingly copied accurately and correctly. Emphasize that enough scrolls have survived through thousands of years to help substantiate the validity of the individual books of the Old Testament as well as the gospels and letters of the New Testament.

23. Encourage Muslims to read the Holy Bible, starting with Genesis and Exodus and then the four gospels (John, Matthew, Mark, and Luke — in that order).

24. Talk about God's requirement of an unblemished blood sacrifice for the forgiveness of sins and how the only perfect blood sacrifice was the one He provided through His *only-begotten* Son, Y'shua H'Moshiach (Jesus the Messiah, or Jesus the Christ).

25. Talk about God's goodness as demonstrated through His grace (receiving from Him what we do not deserve) and mercy (not receiving from Him what we do deserve). God's grace is demonstrated through the opportunity to receive forgiveness for our sins and God's mercy is demonstrated by our not receiving eternal separation from God, which is actually what each one of us does deserve.

26. Talk about how, when we come to the cross of Christ, the burdens of guilt from sin, condemnation by God, and shame are palpably removed from us and that then, and only then, do we have the freedom to be who God created us to be.

APPENDIX D

Instructor Guidelines

Greetings in the precious Name of our Lord and Savior, Jesus Christ!

Islam has significant relevance to Bible students' abilities to interpret end-time events as well as for them to stand firm in their Christian faith even as they are faced with persecution and possible death.

The course entitled "The Antichrist Nature of Islam and the Koran (al-Qur'an)" is meant to be discussion-oriented. If you are taking the course through correspondence, then make sure that you communicate regularly with your facilitator or instructor via email, phone, or post. Each student might even lead small group discussions on the topics contained within this book at the same time that he or she is taking the course.

Following are recommended topics for weekly group discussions that correspond to the sections in this book. If you are taking this course through correspondence, then write an essay for each of the following eleven assignments. (Assignment twelve has its own instructions.)

Foreword

1. Read the entire Book of Revelation and mark each chapter as "chronologically successive" or "conceptually related" to the previous chapter. Explain your reasons for categorizing each chapter as "chronologically successive" or "conceptually related" to its previous chapter.

2. Independent of the existing chapter divisions, organize the Book of Revelation into divisions based on clear distinctions of its various passages.

Chapter One: Introduction

3. What events in history, especially within the past few decades, have shown to the world that Islam is a religion of hatred and intolerance and not a religion of love and peace?

Chapter Two: The Difference between Isaac and Ishmael

4. (a) Using a concordance to your Bible, discuss the descendants of Isaac and Ishmael. (b) Compile an exhaustive list of all Scripture verses that refer to Isaac and Ishmael. (c) Research the meaning of *Eid al-Adha* and discuss how it relates to compromising and delegitimizing Biblical truth.

Chapter Three: The Difference between Jesus and Mohammed

5. Using Scripture (the Holy Bible is the only Scripture), discuss why a so-called "Seal of the Prophets" (i.e., Mohammed): (a) is not necessary for the fulfillment of Bible prophecy; and (b) requires rejection by Christians.

Chapter Four: How It All Adds Up

6. (a) What is the difference between "antichrists" and "the Antichrist?" (b) What are the general characteristics of the end-time Antichrist? (c) Using outside resources (library research tools, Hebrew

internet web pages, local rabbis, etc.), research how numbers are represented in Hebrew and give examples. (There are many websites and published books available on this topic.) (d) Discuss how the final Antichrist will have traits similar to and different from Adolf Hitler. (e) Define *cipher, encryption, encoding, cryptographic, transposition cipher, backward cipher, numeric substitution cipher,* and *mathematic cipher.*

Chapter Five: Interpreting End-Time Prophecy in View of Islam

7. (a) Discuss the general importance of prophecies in Old Testament and New Testament times to current authentic Christian believers. (b) Discuss the specific importance of Bible prophecies that are apocalyptic. (c) Compare and contrast the beasts of Revelation 17 and 13.

Chapter Six: The Worst Woes

8. Discuss the worst woes associated with Trumpet Five, Trumpet Six, and Trumpet Seven.

Chapter Seven: Clarifications concerning the Antichrist

9. (a) Biblically speaking, how will we know when the end-time Antichrist has been revealed? (b) Is it possible that the Antichrist has already assumed power? (c) How is the role of the Antichrist integral to understanding the Tribulation? (Use specific Bible verses to support your statements.)

Chapter Eight: The Fullness of Time

10. Discuss: (a) free will and predestination, (b) God's pure Will and His perfect timing, and (c) the relationship between the Seven Feasts of Israel and the Christian Church by using concepts presented in Appendix B.

Chapter Nine: Human Conflict

11. Discuss the relevance of "turning your other cheek" to protecting yourself and your loved ones from evil in the form of mortal combat.

Assignment 12

12. Based on the number of students that are taking this course, the facilitator/instructor should divide the number of pages in the Koran (al-Qur'an) so that every student is assigned an equal number of pages. Each student is then responsible for reading the pages assigned in order to find at least thirty (30) verses in the Koran that are contradictory to verses in the Holy Bible. After the class takes as many weeks as needed to discuss the chapters in this book, then have each student report on: (a) their individual section(s) of the Koran, (b) the contradictions with the Holy Bible that they found, and (c) why they are contradictions. If students are taking this course through correspondence, each student will be held responsible for selecting thirty (30) verses anywhere in the Koran that are contradictory to verses in the Holy Bible. All students should present their findings using the format shown in Table Nine:

Surah and Verse in the Qur'an	Refutational Bible Citations	Contradiction(s)
Surah 6.032	John 16:33	The Qur'an teaches that "the present life is nothing but a sport and a diversion" for the followers of Allah, but the Bible teaches that "in the world [the followers of Jesus] shall have tribulation."

Answer Format for Assignment Twelve

Table Nine

. . . .

Finally, if the instructor has time, he or she should have a thorough discussion on how Christians can best evangelize Muslims (using Appendix C as well as other resources). Also, the instructor should have the students list current worldwide events that tie into how Satan is using Islam to try to conquer the world.

. . . .

This should be an informal, discussion-oriented class. Evaluation of each student should be determined on classroom participation as well as the extent of each student's research and oral presentations (or written responses to assignments if the course is taken through correspondence).

ENDNOTES

Online Koran (al-Qur´an):
http://corpus.quran.com/translation.jsp?chapter=1&verse=1
Online Bible:
https://www.blueletterbible.org/

1. From *The Koran Interpreted*, by A. J. Arberry, Volume I, Macmillan Publishing Co., Inc., New York, 1955, page 85.
2. Ibid., Volume I, page 44. [brackets mine]
3. Ibid., Volume I, pages 334-335. [brackets mine]
4. Ibid., Volume I, page 83.
5. Ibid., Volume II, page 36. [brackets mine]
6. *Time*, April 16, 1979, page 49.
7. From *Islam*, by Alfred Guillame, Penguin Books Inc., Baltimore, 1956, pages 61-62.
8. Arberry, A. J. Op cit. Volume I, Surah X, page 232. (Surah 10.063-.064)
9. Ibid., Volume I, Surah VI, page 152. (Surah 6.032)
10. Ibid. Volume II, Surah LXVII, page 290. (Surah 67.002)
11. Ibid., Volume I, Surah XI, page 243. [brackets mine] (Surah 11.034)
12. Ibid., Volume I, Surah XIV, page 274 [brackets mine]; see also Volume II: Surah XXXV, page 139; Surah XXXIX, page 168; and Surah XLII, page 197. (Surahs 14.004; 35.008; 39.023; 42.044)
13. Ibid., Volume II, Surah XXI, page 19. (Surah 21.035)
14. Ibid., Volume II, Surah XXIV, page 46. [brackets mine] (Surah 24.002)
15. Ibid., Volume II, Surah LXXVIII, page 321. (Surah 78.031-.034)
16. Ibid., Volume II, Surah XXXVI, page 147. (Surah 36.055-.056)
17. Ibid., Volume II, Surah LXI, page 274. [brackets mine]
18. Ibid., Volume I, page 125.
19. Ibid., Volume I, page 140.
20. Ibid., Volume I, page 125.
21. Ibid., Volume I, page 210.
22. Ibid., Volume I, page 233. [brackets mine]
23. Ibid., Volume I, page 315. [brackets mine]

[24] Ibid., Volume I, page 338.
[25] Ibid., Volume II, page 43. [brackets mine]
[26] Ibid., Volume II, page 56. [brackets mine]
[27] Ibid., Volume II, page 156.
[28] Ibid., Volume II, page 204. [brackets mine]
[29] Ibid.
[30] See also Mark 3:11, 5:7, and Luke 4:41, 8:28
[31] Arberry, A. J. Op cit. Volume I, page 135.
[32] Ibid., Volume II, page 102. [brackets mine]
[33] Ibid., Volume II, page 229. [brackets mine]
[34] Ibid., Volume I, Surah V, page 142; Volume II, Surah XXIV, page 53.
[35] Ibid., Volume I, page 51.
[36] Ibid., Volume I, page 53. [brackets mine]
[37] Ibid., Volume I, page 54.
[38] Ibid., Volume I, page 57.
[39] Ibid., Volume I, page 75. [brackets mine]
[40] Ibid., Volume I, page 133. [brackets mine]
[41] Ibid., Volume I, page 201. [brackets mine]
[42] Ibid., Volume I, page 205.
[43] Ibid., Volume I, page 207.
[44] Ibid., Volume I, page 210. [brackets mine]
[45] Ibid., Volume I, page 211. [brackets mine]
[46] Ibid., Volume I, page 222. [brackets mine]
[47] Ibid., Volume II, page 196.
[48] Ibid., Volume II, page 220. [brackets mine]
[49] Ibid., Volume II, page 229. [brackets mine]
[50] Ibid., Volume II, page 266. [brackets mine]
[51] Ibid., Volume II, page 288.
[52] Ibid., Volume I, page 224. [brackets mine]
[53] Ibid., Volume II, page 106.
[54] Ibid., Volume II, page 134. [brackets mine]
[55] Ibid., Volume II, page 170. [brackets mine]
[56] Ibid., Volume II, page 177. [brackets mine]
[57] Ibid., Volume II, page 246.
[58] Ibid., Volume II, page 279. [brackets mine]
[59] Ibid., Volume I, page 123.
[60] Ibid., Volume I, page 147. [brackets mine]

AFTERWORD

People who worry that nuclear weaponry will one day fall into the hands of radical Muslims fail to realize that the worst Islamic bomb has been dropped already: It fell the day that Mohammed was born.

For those who might think that this book is all doom and gloom, I will close with this sweet chorus of victory:

> Jesus Christ continues to be victorious
> and his followers continue to triumph in him!

Why not read God's Book (the Holy Bible) to find out for yourself how it all ends?

BOOKS BY THE AUTHOR

As I See It: The Nature of Reality by God by Rev. Joseph Adam Pearson, Ph.D., Christ Evangelical Bible Institute, Copyright 2015. ISBN 978-0615590615.

Classroom Version of As I See It: The Nature of Reality by God by Rev. Joseph Adam Pearson, Ph.D., Christ Evangelical Bible Institute, Copyright 2019. ISBN: 978-1734294705.

God, Our Universal Self: A Primer for Future Christian Metaphysics by Rev. Joseph Adam Pearson, Ph.D., Christ Evangelical Bible Institute, Copyright 2020. ISBN 978-0985772857.

Divine Metaphysics of Human Anatomy by Rev. Joseph Adam Pearson, Ph.D., Christ Evangelical Bible Institute, Copyright 2018. ISBN 978-0985772819.

Hello from 3050 AD! by Rev. Joseph Adam Pearson, Ph.D., Christ Evangelical Bible Institute, Copyright 2019. ISBN 978-0996222402.

Christianity and Homosexuality Reconciled: New Thinking for a New Millennium! by Rev. Joseph Adam Pearson, Ph.D., Christ Evangelical Bible Institute, Copyright 2021. ISBN 978-0985772888.

The Koran (al-Qur'an): Testimony of Antichrist by Rev. Joseph Adam Pearson, Ph.D., Christ Evangelical Bible Institute, Copyright 2021. ISBN 978-0985772833.

Telugu Version of Quran: Testimony of Antichrist by Rev. Joseph Adam Pearson, Ph.D., Christ Evangelical Bible Institute, Copyright 2020. ISBN 978-0996222457.

Urdu Version of Quran: Testimony of Antichrist by Rev. Joseph Adam Pearson, Ph.D., Christ Evangelical Bible Institute, Copyright 2020. ISBN 978-0996222440.

Revelation of Antichrist by Rev. Joseph Adam Pearson, Ph.D., Christ Evangelical Bible Institute, Copyright 2021. ISBN 978-0996222488.

Intelligent Evolution by Rev. Joseph Adam Pearson, Ph.D., Christ Evangelical Bible Institute, Copyright 2020. ISBN 978-0996222426.

The Biology of Psychism from a Christian Perspective by Rev. Joseph Adam Pearson, Ph.D., Christ Evangelical Bible Institute, Copyright 2020. ISBN 978-0996222464.

The Threeness of God by Rev. Joseph Adam Pearson, Ph.D., Christ Evangelical Bible Institute, Copyright 2020. ISBN 978-1734294729.

To access free pdf and mobi editions of Dr. Pearson's books, visit
http://www.christevangelicalbibleinstitute.com
or
http://www.dr-joseph-adam-pearson.com

BOOKS BY THE AUTHOR

As I See It: The Nature of Reality by God by Rev. Joseph Adam Pearson, Ph.D., Christ Evangelical Bible Institute, Copyright 2015. ISBN 978-0615590615.

Classroom Version of As I See It: The Nature of Reality by God by Rev. Joseph Adam Pearson, Ph.D., Christ Evangelical Bible Institute, Copyright 2019. ISBN: 978-1734294705.

God, Our Universal Self: A Primer for Future Christian Metaphysics by Rev. Joseph Adam Pearson, Ph.D., Christ Evangelical Bible Institute, Copyright 2020. ISBN 978-0985772857.

Divine Metaphysics of Human Anatomy by Rev. Joseph Adam Pearson, Ph.D., Christ Evangelical Bible Institute, Copyright 2018. ISBN 978-0985772819.

Hello from 3050 AD! by Rev. Joseph Adam Pearson, Ph.D., Christ Evangelical Bible Institute, Copyright 2019. ISBN 978-0996222402.

Christianity and Homosexuality Reconciled: New Thinking for a New Millennium! by Rev. Joseph Adam Pearson, Ph.D., Christ Evangelical Bible Institute, Copyright 2021. ISBN 978-0985772888.

The Koran (al-Qur'an): Testimony of Antichrist by Rev. Joseph Adam Pearson, Ph.D., Christ Evangelical Bible Institute, Copyright 2021. ISBN 978-0985772833.

Telugu Version of Quran: Testimony of Antichrist by Rev. Joseph Adam Pearson, Ph.D., Christ Evangelical Bible Institute, Copyright 2020. ISBN 978-0996222457.

Urdu Version of Quran: Testimony of Antichrist by Rev. Joseph Adam Pearson, Ph.D., Christ Evangelical Bible Institute, Copyright 2020. ISBN 978-0996222440.

Revelation of Antichrist by Rev. Joseph Adam Pearson, Ph.D., Christ Evangelical Bible Institute, Copyright 2021. ISBN 978-0996222488.

Intelligent Evolution by Rev. Joseph Adam Pearson, Ph.D., Christ Evangelical Bible Institute, Copyright 2020. ISBN 978-0996222426.

The Biology of Psychism from a Christian Perspective by Rev. Joseph Adam Pearson, Ph.D., Christ Evangelical Bible Institute, Copyright 2020. ISBN 978-0996222464.

The Threeness of God by Rev. Joseph Adam Pearson, Ph.D., Christ Evangelical Bible Institute, Copyright 2020. ISBN 978-1734294729.

To access free pdf and mobi editions of Dr. Pearson's books, visit
http://www.christevangelicalbibleinstitute.com
or
http://www.dr-joseph-adam-pearson.com

ABOUT THE AUTHOR

Dr. Joseph Adam Pearson is a college and university educator with more than forty years of classroom and administrative experience. Dr. Pearson has been the International President and Chief Executive Officer of Christ Evangelical Bible Institute (CEBI) for over twenty years. At the time of the latest publication of this book (2021), he still oversees thriving branch campuses of CEBI in India, Pakistan, and Tanzania.

Currently, Dr. Pearson spends the majority of his time developing, designing, and deploying curriculum for Christian education nationally and internationally. And he preaches, teaches, and leads international crusades as well as provides group pastoral training in global mission settings.

During his professional life, Dr. Pearson has also served in the role of Senior Pastor of Healing Waters Ministries in Tempe, Arizona and as Dean of Instruction for Mesa Community College in Mesa, Arizona — where he was founding instructional dean for its Red Mountain Campus as well as Director of its Extended Campus.

Dr. Pearson holds a Bachelor of Science degree in Biology from Loyola University (Chicago), a Master of Science degree in Biology from Loyola University (Chicago), and a Ph.D. in Curriculum and Instruction with specializations in language, literacy, linguistics, and textual analysis from Arizona State University. He has also taken additional doctoral level coursework at the University of Chicago and at the University of Illinois Medical Center.

Dr. Pearson believes that after we are saved, and at the same time we are being sanctified, our individual lives and deeds are part of an "application" for the jobs that we will each hold during Christ Jesus' Millennial reign on Earth. Dr. Pearson's greatest goal is to be one of the many committed Christian educators who will be teaching during that period of time.

You may contact Dr. Pearson at drjpearson@aol.com and drjosephadampearson@gmail.com

www.ingramcontent.com/pod-product-compliance
Lightning Source LLC
Chambersburg PA
CBHW081456040426

42446CB00016B/3269